access to

in depth

HITLER, APPEASEMENT
and the ROAD TO WAR
1933 – 41

Graham Darby

Hodder & Stoughton

A MEMBER OF THE HODDER HEADLINE GROUP

Acknowledgements

The author and the publisher would like to thank the following for permission to reproduce copyright illustrations herein: p. 33 and p. 96, David Low, *Evening Standard* © Solo Syndication and Centre for the Study of Cartoons and Caricature, University of Kent at Canterbury; p. 65, Will Dyson, *Daily Herald* and Centre for the Study of Cartoons and Caricature, University of Kent at Canterbury; p. 77, bottom, Gabriel; p. 92, Illustrated London News; p. 94 David King Collection. All other photos supplied by the publisher.

Orders: please contact Bookpoint Ltd, 39 Milton Park, Abingdon, Oxon OX14 4TD. Telephone: (44) 01235 400414, Fax: (44) 01235 400454. Lines are open from 9.00 - 6.00, Monday to Saturday, with a 24 hour message answering service. Email address: orders@bookpoint.co.uk

British Library Cataloguing in Publication Data
A catalogue for this title is available from the British Library

ISBN 0 340 746 971

First published 1999

Impression number	10	9	8	7	6	5	4	3	2	1
Year			2004	2003	2002	2001	2000	1999		

Copyright © 1999 Graham Darby

Cover illustration provided by AKG photos

Typeset by Sempringham publishing services, Bedford
Printed in Great Britain for Hodder & Stoughton Educational, a division of Hodder Headline Plc, 338 Euston Road, London NW1 3BH by Redwood Books, Trowbridge, Wiltshire.

Contents

Preface

The original *Access to History* series was conceived as a collection of sets of books covering popular chronological periods in British history, such as 'the Tudors' and 'the nineteenth century', together with the histories of other countries, such as France, Germany, Russia and the USA. This arrangement complemented the way in which early modern and modern history has traditionally been taught in sixth forms, colleges and universities. In recent years, however, other ways of dividing up the past have become increasingly popular. In particular, there has been a greater emphasis on studying relatively brief periods in considerable detail and on comparing similar historical phenomena in different countries. These developments have generated a demand for appropriate learning materials, and, in response, two new 'strands' are being added to the main series - *In Depth* and *Themes*. The new volumes build directly on the features that have made *Access to History* so popular.

To the general reader

Although *Access* books have been specifically designed to meet the needs of examination students, these volumes also have much to offer the general reader. *Access* authors are committed to the belief that good history must not only be accurate, up-to-date and scholarly, but also clearly and attractively written. The main body of the text (excluding the 'Study Guides') should, therefore, form a readable and engaging survey of a topic. Moreover, each author has aimed not merely to provide as clear an explanation as possible of what happened in the past but also to stimulate readers and to challenge them into thinking for themselves about the past and its significance. Thus, although no prior knowledge is expected from the reader, he or she is treated as an intelligent and thinking person throughout. The author tends to share ideas and explore possibilities, instead of delivering so-called 'historical truths' from on high.

To the student reader

It is intended that *Access* books should be used by students studying history at a higher level. Its volumes are all designed to be working texts, which should be reasonably clear on a first reading but which will benefit from re-reading and close study. To be an effective and successful student, you need to budget your time wisely. Hence you should think carefully about how important the material in a particular book is for you. If you simply need to acquire a general grasp of a topic, the following approach will probably be effective:

1. Read Chapter 1, which should give you an overview of the whole book, and think about its contents.

2. Skim through Chapter 2, paying particular attention to the opening section and to the headings and sub-headings. Decide if you need to read the whole chapter.
3. If you do, read the chapter, stopping at the end of every sub-division of the text to make notes.
4. Repeat stage 2 (and stage 3 where appropriate) for the other chapters.

If, however, your course - and your particular approach to it - demands a detailed knowledge of the contents of the book, you will need to be correspondingly more thorough. There is no perfect way of studying, and it is particularly worthwhile experimenting with different styles of note-making to find the one that best suits you. Nevertheless, the following plan of action is worth trying:

1. Read a whole chapter quickly, preferably at one sitting. Avoid the temptation - which may be very great - to make notes at this stage.
2. Study the flow diagram at the end of the chapter, ensuring that you understand the general 'shape' of what you have read.
3. Re-read the chapter more slowly, this time taking notes. You may well be amazed at how much more intelligible and straightforward the material seems on a second reading - and your notes will be correspondingly more useful to you when you have to write an essay or revise for an exam. In the long run, reading a chapter twice can, in fact, often save time. Be sure to make your notes in a clear, orderly fashion, and spread them out so that, if necessary, you can later add extra information.
4. Read the advice on essay questions, and do tackle the specimen titles. (Remember that if learning is to be effective, it must be active. No one - alas - has yet devised any substitute for real effort. It is up to you to make up your own mind on the key issues in any topic.)
5. Attempt the source-based questions. The guidance on tackling these exercises, which is generally given at least once in a book, is well worth reading and thinking about.

When you have finished the main chapters, go through the 'Further Reading' section. Remember that no single book can ever do more than introduce a topic, and it is to be hoped that - time permitting - you will want to read more widely. If *Access* books help you to discover just how diverse and fascinating the human past can be, the series will have succeeded in its aim - and you will experience that enthusiasm for the subject which, along with efficient learning, is the hallmark of all the best students.

Robert Pearce

1 Introduction

POINTS TO CONSIDER

This chapter will introduce you to the historiography of the topic and some of the key questions that have been generated. It will then go on to give you an outline of the book's content and an outline of the period 1919-1933. Your aim will be to keep the key questions in mind as well as the important events of 1919-1933 which form the context for the later years.

KEY DATES

1919	Paris Peace Settlement
1921	Reparations fixed at 132 billion gold marks
1922	Treaty of Rapallo between Germany and the USSR
1923	French occupation of the Ruhr
1924	Dawes Plan
1925	Locarno Treaty
1926	Germany joins the League of Nations
1929	Young Plan; the Wall Street Crash
1930	Allied evacuation of the Rhineland
1931	Japan invades Manchuria
1932	Reparations virtually abolished; Disarmament Conference
1933	Hitler comes to power and Japan leaves the League of Nations

1 The Key Questions

> KEY ISSUE How have historians' views on the origins of the Second World War changed over time and what questions does this debate raise?

The explanation for the origins of the Second World War used to be a relatively straightforward matter: the (innocent) western democracies had been attacked by a ruthless, expansionist Germany. Unlike the First World War, where there was considerable scope for debate about origins and responsibility, the Second World War seemed easily explained. Germany provoked the war to reverse the verdict of the last one, destroy the Treaty of Versailles and win continental hegemony. More than that, the conflict was largely due to one man, the German Chancellor and leader of the Nazi party, Adolf Hitler. He and his cronies planned the war and brought it about. Accordingly, this was the principal charge brought against captured Nazis at the Nuremberg trials in 1946 - that they had conspired to bring about an aggressive war.

So, in the light of this diagnosis, was the Second World War inevitable? Perhaps, perhaps not - there was also an alternative explanation. For despite Hitler's ruthless determination, was it conceivably a war that could have been avoided - an 'unnecessary war' in the words of Winston Churchill?[1] Part of this argument was a list of 'lost opportunities' to stop Hitler - for instance, in the Rhineland in 1936, or at Munich in 1938. Had Chamberlain not appeased, had France been more decisive, had the Soviet Union not collaborated, had the USA not been isolationist, then, the argument went, the war would have been less likely to occur. But occur it did, and this speculation did not alter the picture that much: Hitler was still responsible. The avoidable war and the inevitable war could be reconciled. Hitler planned the war, so the argument goes, but the democracies did play a part in failing to stop him. Thus what was avoidable at one time became inevitable later.

Although there was not always complete consensus, these explanations by and large held sway until A.J.P. Taylor turned everything upside down with his book *The Origins of the Second World War* in 1961. Taylor saw Hitler not as an evil monster bent on world domination but as an ordinary German statesman whose policy was not dissimilar to that of his predecessors. At the same time the German historian Fritz Fischer[2] also stressed the continuity of aims between the Second and Third Reichs, comparing Bethmann Hollweg's September Programme (the secret memorandum of 1914 which called for a German-dominated Mitteleuropa, i.e. Central Europe) and Brest-Litovsk (the harsh peace treaty with Russia signed in March 1918) with Hitler's writings. For Taylor the Second World War was not so much Hitler's war as a re-run of 1914-18. It was a case of old-fashioned balance-of-power politics, in which the powers vied with each other in a struggle for the mastery of Europe. Moreover, Britain and France were not wholly innocent; they too were governed by *raison d'état* (literally 'reason of state', what was best for the state) rather than moral considerations: they were equally self-interested. Thus if British and French policies were self-serving, then in this context appeasement, the much criticised policy of making concessions, also took on a different light - perhaps it was the most appropriate policy at the time and a way of buying time (the debate on appeasement will be dealt with in Chapter 5). And it must be remembered that Britain and France declared war on Germany, not the other way round.

Central to Taylor's thesis was his belief that Hitler was simply an opportunist and not a planner. Responding to this contention, Alan Bullock in the second edition of his biography (1962) confirmed Hitler's opportunism but also highlighted his plans to overthrow Versailles and achieve German domination of Europe. He resolved this apparent contradiction by seeing him as an opportunist in the short term, but a planner in the long term. Still others preferred to see Hitler solely as a planner and ascribed to him a blueprint for action (e.g. William Shirer in his best seller of 1960 *The Rise and Fall of the Third Reich*), a contention borne out by the regularity of his moves, the systematic way he went from one demand to another (each being 'positively my last' ...!). Hugh Trevor Roper suggested that Hitler's planning went beyond Versailles and hegemony: *lebensraum* (living space) was his fundamental aim, and this required a war of conquest. However, Taylor saw only opportunism and dismissed the idea of any plan at all. The Hossbach Memorandum (1937) for instance, he described, as 'day-dreaming' (see page 48): 'there was no concrete plan', was his conclusion.

Taylor's book caused quite a stir at the time, generating more vitriol (hostile remarks) than endorsement, but it did spawn debate, a new look at the origins of the war, an end to complacency and a plethora of new research and writing which made it clear that the picture was really more complex than had been thought hitherto.

Subsequently, in the late 1960s, historians began to divide into two schools of thought, the *intentionalists* on the one hand and *functionalists* or structuralists on the other. For the *intentionalists* Hitler remains central to the origins of the war. Many identify a clear *intention* to wage war based on the ideas of racial supremacy and the acquisition of a German world empire outlined in his writings. But whether or not you subscribe to the idea that Hitler had a plan, it was still his dictatorial will that was the determining factor in the foreign policy of the Third Reich, in the drive to war. *Intentionalists* include the historians Klaus Hildebrand,[3] Andreas Hillgruber, and Eberhard Jäckel.

Functionalists,[4] on the other hand, believe that foreign policy was created by the economic and social conditions of the Third Reich: it was determined by the structure of the state - and that structure was an anarchy of competing agencies. Hitler was in fact a weak dictator and the Nazi administration was chaotic; hence Nazi policy was reactive. This harked back to Taylor. Hans Mommsen reiterated the fact that Hitler had no plan and Martin Brozat saw *lebensraum* not as a concrete goal but as an ideological metaphor - an image to aim for, to justify unceasing foreign policy intitiatives. Tim Mason contended that the war occurred as a result of the domestic, economic crisis in Germany in the late 1930s. He stated that, by June 1941,'it was clear that the German war economy would have collapsed in 1939/40 if the occupied areas had not been looted of raw materials, foodstuffs, war *matérial* and production capacity.'[5] Basically what he meant is that the German economy could not continue to expand or even function at the same capacity without plundering neighbouring states - Hitler had to expand the Reich to avoid economic disaster. Rearmament and the expense of public works could not be sustained indefinitely.

But just as Taylor's work did not achieve acceptance (and has subsequently been shown to be flawed in a number of crucial areas) so too the *functionalists* have not really had the best of the debate. Although their researches have enriched our historical knowledge of the functioning of the Third Reich, there is difficulty in demonstrating how social and economic factors influenced the formation of foreign policy. Indeed there is hardly any evidence at all to show that they did. For most observers the *intentionalists* are more convincing and the title of this book is a reflection of that fact.

But if 'the centrality of Hitler and German policy to the origins of the war is little questioned by historians',[6] there are nevertheless a number of key questions thrown up by all this historical debate, and ones which will have to be addressed in the course of this book. Among them are:

- How much continuity was there between the foreign policies of the Second(1871-1918) and Third(1933-1945) Reichs? Was Hitler little different from his predecessors? Were his aims the same as the Kaiser's in 1914? Or Stresemann's in the 1920s?
- Was Hitler an opportunist or a planner? Did he have a blueprint, a timetable which he followed? Did Nazi ideology make the war inevitable? Did Hitler get the war he wanted or did it come about by accident?
- Could Hitler have been stopped at any stage prior to 1939? Was the war avoidable?
- Did he intend a series of short wars or a much larger war, starting in the 1940s? What do Nazi economic and rearmament policies tell us about his intentions?
- Who was morally responsible for the outbreak of the war? How much blame should be allotted to Hitler, to the Nazis, to the German people, to Britain, France, and the Soviet Union? In this context, was Appeasement a cowardly policy that only encouraged Hitler? Or was it an honourable policy, or the only policy open to the democracies?

2 General Outline

> **KEY ISSUE** What are the major issues under discussion in this book?

This book will concentrate on the years 1933 to 1939 and will focus on all the major powers involved. However, given the centrality of Hitler's role, we will mainly focus on his actions and the reaction of the major powers to those actions.

(a) Early Years

Initially we will look at the origins and sources for Hitler's thinking, his writings and his speeches. We will look at the centrality of 'race' and 'space' in his foreign policy objectives. Initially, in the years 1933-35, his position was weak, but even so he was able to exploit allied disunity and accelerate rearmament and introduce conscription.

(b) Diplomatic Revolution

Something of a diplomatic revolution occurred between 1935 and 1937 as Mussolini, hitherto a potential ally of the democracies and wary of Hitler, was condemned for his attack on Abyssinia by Britain and France and reacted by making a deal with the German dictator. The League of Nations was further discredited and Hitler took advantage of the situation to remilitarise the Rhineland (1936). The Spanish Civil War also brought the dictators closer together and the Rome-Berlin Axis (an understanding between Nazi Germany and Fascist Italy) was formed at the end of the year.

(c) Hitler Changes Gear 1937-8

Now the balance of power had been altered, Hitler began to take the inititiative. The Hossbach Memorandum of 1937 (the record of a four-hour meeting in which Hitler outlined his plans to his top brass) should be seen in this context and should be taken seriously, contrary to A.J.P. Taylor's objections. The Generals who objected were soon removed and there followed the *Anschluss* (union) with Austria in March 1938. The timing was not Hitler's, but the democracies' acquiescence was a lesson not lost on the German dictator. The partition of Czechoslovakia, conceded by the democracies at Munich, followed in September.

(d) Appeasement

Clearly Hitler increasingly took the initiative, but it is essential that students appreciate the problems faced by the democracies. France was not only affected by a strong strain of pacificism but was in fact economically and militarily weak, and largely dependent on Great Britain. British policy was very much determined by her global commitments and global vulnerability. These considerations, taken together with a feeling of sympathy for some revision of Versailles, render British policy intelligible. Seen in this light Appeasement looks like a rational policy based on what was possible. However, it was only compromise up to a point, as the historiographical debate on Chamberlain will show.

(e) The Outbreak of War 1939

After Munich Hitler broke his promises and occupied the rest of Czechoslovakia. Britain and France's guarantees to Poland in March 1939 were intended to be a warning to Hitler to desist. Even before the occupation of Prague a decision had been reached to draw a line in the sand. However, the democracies' antipathy towards Stalin enabled Hitler to pull off a remarkable diplomatic coup with the Nazi

Soviet Pact in August 1939. Hitler pressed ahead with his invasion of Poland on September 1st convinced that he had avoided a general war.

He was wrong, but quite why Britain and France decided to make a stand at this point will be investigated. The war went badly for the democracies; Hitler won a rapid and remarkable victory in the West in the summer of 1940. However, for Hitler this military triumph was really only a sideshow. The main aim remained *lebensraum*, and Operation Barbarossa, the invasion of Russia in 1941, was the prelude to a new racial order. Arguably everything had been leading up to this point.

Accordingly there is a very good case for laying the responsibility for the War at the feet of Hitler. However, it would be facile to blame just one man. Hitler was not operating in a vacuum; he was in fact operating in a most favourable climate, and it is to this broader context that we must now turn. Without defeat in World War One, without the humiliation of Versailles and without the collapse of the world economy at the time of the Depression, it is inconceivable that Adolf Hitler could have come to power.

3 The Weaknesses of the Paris Peace Settlement

> **KEY ISSUE** What mistakes were made in drawing up the peace settlement in 1919?

For many observers the Second World War was a rerun of the First. Put simply, the side that had begun the conflict in 1914 lost, and tried to reverse that decision in 1939. Proponents of this view see the inadequacy of the Treaty of Versailles as fundamental, contending that the settlement fell between two stools, arguably too harsh and too soft at the same time.

The collapse of the German war effort in November 1918 was sudden and unexpected, coming as a surprise to both the allies and the German people. After all, earlier in the year Russia had finally acknowledged defeat athe German army had launched a fresh offensive that had again taken her forces close to Paris: the German people anticipated victory. Although this offensive had failed by the summer and the Germans had been pushed back, they had not been defeated and the allies were making firm arrangements for 1919 and even talking of war lasting into 1920. Thus the sudden end to the war in November 1918 caught everyone unprepared.

Indeed the way the war ended, with the German army intact and Germany unoccupied, served to hide what had really happened and led to false assumptions in Germany. Firstly, there was the belief that the war had been ended by the Germans prematurely in order to obtain a soft peace based on Wilson's 14 points (a peace programme put forward by the American president in January 1918); and secondly, when that peace turned out not to be soft, there developed the myth that the army had not been defeated at all but had been 'stabbed in the back' and betrayed by democratic and socialist politicians. The fact that both these assumptions are wrong is irrelevant because they do help to explain the German attitude to the peace settlement.

The suddenness of the end of war meant that the Treaty of Versailles was cobbled together and signed in great haste and confusion. In effect it was the work of three men, President Wilson of the USA and the Prime Ministers of Britain and France, Lloyd George and Clemenceau. The portrayal of their positions as idealism, pragmatism and revenge respectively is undoubtedly an oversimplification, but it is nevertheless a useful characterisation. The 'big three' were under tremendous pressure and worked without an agenda, and with imperfect information, in a hectic six week period. They had to strike deals; they had to compromise. However, to suggest as some commentators do, that the peacemakers faced appalling if not insurmountable difficulties, and did quite well in the circumstances might be a fair point to make, but it only serves to reinforce the judgment that it *was* an imperfect peace.

It is clear that the Treaty of Versailles was neither soft enough to reconcile the Germans, nor harsh enough to cripple them forever: it fell between two stools. It left Germany with grievances and the latent power to make trouble in the future. In fact it was felt to be a stunning blow to German pride. First of all the Germans resented the fact that the peace was a *diktat* - that is to say it was a dictated peace: there was simply no time for consultation. They resented the War Guilt Clause (Article 231), though many historians now believe, as the peacemakers did then, that the Germans were responsible for the war (though of course the men of the Kaiser's government who had taken the decisions in 1914 were no longer in charge). They resented Reparations, though in truth the delay in fixing the amount (until 1921) worked in Germany's favour and only a trivial sum was ever paid. They resented the loss of territory - 13 per cent of land and 10 per cent of population, as well as all colonies - but in truth the Germans themselves would have imposed a much harsher peace on their defeated enemies (their September Programme envisaged massive annexations) if they had won. They also resented the fact that the principle of national determination was adopted at the peace settlement for all peoples except Germans (millions of Germans were now in Poland and Czechoslovakia, and a further 7 million in Austria). This simply served to regenerate and perpetuate a sense of wounded racial pride in Germany. The emasculation of Germany's armed forces (limited to an army of 100,000 men, no airforce, only six capital ships etc) was humiliating for a country with such a strong military tradition, but easily evaded (the military inspectorate was

European frontiers 1919-37

withdrawn in 1927 as a gesture of goodwill!) and Germany remained potentially strong. The French position, advocating a Rhine border, an independent Rhineland state and the League of Nations as a military alliance made a lot of sense - and perhaps the other extreme (a more idealistic settlement) made sense too. However, the truth is that just as the Germans did not accept that they had caused the war so too they questioned whether they had truly lost it. As we have already indicated, it was the defeat itself that the German people found so hard to accept. Thus any peace treaty which treated Germany as the defeated party was bound to be unacceptable to the German people.

Of course it is true to say that a great number of the treaty clauses were flawed - putting a time limit of 15 years on the occupation of the Rhineland was storing up trouble for the future (though permanent occupation was obviously not a viable alternative either) and the creation of new states in central and eastern Europe led to chronic destabilisation and a power vacuum conducive to German expansion - but perhaps it was really the failure to enforce the Treaty that was the nub of the problem. And the reason for this was the subsequent breakdown of consensus - all three architects of the peace treaty were soon out of office. Wilson had a stroke later in 1919 and Congress refused to ratify the Treaty; Lloyd George hung on to 1922 but the British soon came to see the peace as too harsh and favoured some revision; Clemenceau fell at the beginning of 1920 and although French policy remained consistently hostile to Germany for the time being, the collapse of consensus meant that France was left very much in the lurch - with a colossal debt and little security. Germany's population of 60 million still looked pretty formidable to France's 40 million, and it is clear that, for France, Versailles failed to solve the threat posed by Germany's natural predominance in Europe. After all, Germany had not been scarred by occupation in the war and the 1914 barriers to expansion in the East were now gone.

Inevitably the peace was a compromise and it turned out to be a strange cocktail of Wilsonian idealism (e.g. the League of Nations and the principle of self-determination), French revenge (reparations, war guilt etc) and British pragmatism (temporary occupation of the Saar and Rhineland, plebiscite over the neutrality of Danzig, the partition of Silesia). But the real problems were created by the Treaties of St. Germain (with Austria) and Trianon (with Hungary), which meant that Germany was now surrounded by weak states. Of course Poland, Czechoslovakia and Yugoslavia were not created by the peace settlement but merely recognised by it. And given the fact that eastern Europe and the Balkans were 'a bewildering kaleidoscope of races and religion,'[7] it is hardly surprising that within the new states there were minority groups who did not want to be there and who looked to a neighbouring state for protection. The opportunities for a sufficiently powerful state to disrupt the new order were obvious. Gone was the stabilising influence of the Habsburg Empire, which had somehow kept these ethnic tensions in balance - and gone too was Tsarist Russia. In the east there now lurked the Soviet Union, initially weak but with a new form of government which threatened to undermine the established order. And it should also be remembered that Germany was not the only dissatisfied power: Hungary, the above-mentioned USSR and even Italy were not happy with the outcome. The Paris Peace Settlement created as many problems as it solved. Yet, as we have already stated, it was the failure to enforce the peace terms that really undermined the settlement.

4 Keeping the Peace

KEY ISSUE Why were the terms of the peace not enforced?

First of all it is important to remember that the First World War was the most destructive war there had ever been. Thus regardless of the specific terms of the peace settlement, the war had in many ways created a new, unstable world in which economies had been distorted and traditional ruling systems swept away. It had also had a considerable psychological impact. The new situation was fluid, the potential for danger considerable. In these circumstances any peace settlement might fail and there was no shortage of Jeremiahs who were prepared to say as much.

Marshal Foch, the French commander of the Allied armies, condemned the Versailles settlement as 'an armistice for twenty years'. This proved to be remarkably prescient, but we should remember that the Second World War was not inevitable from this point. After all, either the peace had to be enforced or, failing that, there had to be a revision of its terms and a genuine reconciliation. But to achieve either of these there had to be a common approach by the powers. Unfortunately consensus and cooperation were the first casualties in the post-war period.

The successful implementation of the peace very much depended upon the involvement of the United States. However, her failure to ratify the treaties and withdrawal into, if not isolation, then indifference unhinged the settlement from the very start. No doubt had Britain and France been able to agree on a common policy, the settlement of 1919 might have served as a basis for a lasting peace but unfortunately they could not. Britain was preoccupied with her imperial commitments and soon favoured a revision of the peace, while France alone favoured its rigid implementation. In truth of course both these powers had been seriously weakened by the war and had come to depend on the United States. They were not strong enough to enforce the peace in all its aspects.

From the very beginning the Germans were disinclined to comply with the treaty terms and in 1922 actually made a covert deal with the

Russians at Rapallo to disguise rearmament (economic co-operation was a cover for military co-operation). At the end of that year another default on reparation payments led to a French and Belgian occupation of the Ruhr in January 1923. This had the most serious consequences - not just for Germany, where hyperinflation wreaked havoc on the middle class, but for France, which found herself isolated. In this sense the Ruhr occupation was very much a defeat for the French. The crisis was eventually resolved by the USA, which by the Dawes Plan rescheduled Germany's payments and obtained loans for her. This clearly undermined Versailles and French policy and was a settlement favourable to Germany. Indeed it was the US insistence on debt repayment that made reparation payments so vital for France and poisoned European relations throughout the 1920s.

In 1919 France had been led to believe she would receive Anglo-American military guarantees. However, these did not materialise once Congress rejected the treaties. Hence she made a number of bilateral agreements, with Poland in 1921 and with Czechoslovakia in 1924, but these offered her little security; some might say the contrary as she was committed to their protection. From 1920 to 1925 France tried and failed to obtain a military alliance with Great Britain. In the absence of an agreement, French leaders would not contemplate any revision of the peace settlement or any form of disarmament. They also tried to beef up the League of Nations, but again Britain would not cooperate. Britain could not afford European military commitments when it had so many imperial ones; and, in any event, now that Germany no longer had a navy or an empire, she was no longer seen as a major threat.

In 1925 the Germans offered a treaty to guarantee the western frontiers as laid down by the Versailles Treaty. Britain and France took up this opportunity. At the time the Locarno Treaty was hailed as a diplomatic triumph, and the following year Germany joined the League of Nations, an act of symbolic reconciliation. However, the powers perceived the Treaty in different ways: for France it seemed to represent Germany's reconciliation to Versailles and a firm commitment from Great Britain; for Great Britain it was the limit of her commitment; and for Germany it was the beginning of the revision of Versailles. Moreover, it was significant that similar guarantees were not made for the frontiers of eastern Europe; Locarno in effect wrote off Versailles in that part of the world. Once again this was a treaty that favoured Germany. Under the pressures created by Dawes and Locarno, French policy went on the defensive (the Maginot line - a line of defensive fortifications along the Franco-German border - was approved in 1925 though not begun until 1929) and was transformed from one of coercion to one of exaggerated *détente* (reconciliation). However, 'instead of reconciling Germany to Versailles ... *détente* increased German impatience and accelerated demands for further revision.'[8] Indeed Stresemann, who is often misleadingly described as that fine, moderate statesman of the Weimar era, wanted allied evacuation of the Rhineland, the return of Eupen-Malmedy, of the Saar, of the colonies, the incorporation of Austria and even the return of Alsace Lorraine (though much of this was kept secret).

The Locarno honeymoon (and US loans) only served to mask potential diplomatic instability and continuing German dissatisfaction. Successive German governments in the 1920s made it clear that they did not accept the eastern territorial settlement as permanent; successive German governments clandestinely rearmed (Rapallo was renewed with the Soviets in Berlin in 1926); and successive German governments continued to bleat about reparations - to such an extent that repayments were considerably scaled down by another plan, the Young Plan in 1929. At this time the allies also agreed to evacuate the Rhineland the following year. When the Depression struck later in October 1929 and ended this short period of cooperation, differences about how to apply or revise the peace remained unresolved. For Locarno to have worked it had to be accompanied by a series of negotiated concessions to Germany. French disinclination to make revisions was well known; however, between 1924 and 1929 British foreign policy under Austen Chamberlain also became markedly less sympathetic to the German position. 'The failure of the architects of the 1919 peace settlement to complete their work on an agreed basis in the decade after 1919 was one of the major factors contributing to the outbreak of war [in 1939].'[9] However, we must not be tempted to read history backwards. Were the hopes of Locarno illusory? We will never know. The Wall Street Crash and the World Depression cut off all hopes of recovery. And it was the Depression that brought Hitler to power.

5 Economic Collapse and Diplomatic Instability

> **KEY ISSUE** What effect did the Great Depression have on an already unstable international system?

Whatever its causes the Depression which began in 1929 led to the collapse of international trade, a crisis in credit and banking and large-scale unemployment. All countries were forced to try to protect their own interests, and this in turn caused growing friction, an economic free-for-all and a search for self-sufficiency. The economic recovery in Europe had been excessively dependent on American loans which operated in a triangular fashion. Basically, Germany borrowed from the US to help pay reparations to Britain, France and Italy, and they in turn paid the money back to the US to service war debts. With the collapse of US credit and the calling-in of short-term loans, this cycle was broken. Germany was particularly hard hit as she had borrowed more than she had ever paid in reparations, and many of her loans were short-term. By May 1932 unemployment there had reached 6 million (30 per cent of the workforce), and this fed feelings of frustrated nationalism. With regard to the revision of Versailles, it was increasingly suggested that what could not be obtained by negotiation should be demanded as a matter of right. In this atmosphere a large proportion of the German middle class, fearing another 1923 (the year of hyperinflation and ruin for many) and fearing communist revolution, turned to the Nazi party. Arguably the advent to power of Hitler was the most far-reaching consequence of the Depression.

Another of its consequences was the Japanese invasion of Manchuria in 1931. Although militant nationalism had been growing in the Japanese Empire for some time, the loss of jobs and the collapse in rice and silk prices reinforced the position of the right-wing military faction. However, the real significance of the invasion was that it fully exposed the weaknesses of the League of Nations. Without Russian and US participation, and without an army of its own, the League had always been weak, though it had been able to resolve disputes between minor powers. The League was in effect controlled by Britain and France but they often steered it in different directions. In many ways the weaknesses of the League were a reflection of the weaknesses of the democracies. Britain and France were not prepared to do anything against Japan, so when the League condemned the Japanese, Japan simply ignored the League altogether and walked out. This hardly inspired confidence for the future and was not an auspicious context for the Disarmament Conference, a legacy of the *détente* years, which opened in 1932. French refusal to disarm was an opportunity for Germany to demand the right to rearm (see page 22).

By 1933 Germany had in fact secured a substantial revision of the Treaty of Versailles - she was a member of the League of Nations, rearmament was no longer subject to scrutiny, the Rhineland had been evacuated and finally reparations had been in effect cancelled (at Lausanne in 1932) - but it had been achieved 'in a way that caused apprehension in France, irritation in GB and resentment in Germany.'[10] This was the context in which Hitler came to power in 1933.

The Great Depression itself clearly did not lead directly to war - war came after recovery was well under way - but its effects were far-reaching. It destroyed the positive and encouraging economic and political developments of the years between 1924 and 1930. Franco-German cooperation and the 'spirit of Locarno' fizzled out. Indeed by 1933 the hopes engendered by Locarno seemed a distant dream. Thus the background to our main period of focus is:

i)   a flawed peace settlement
ii) no agreed means of its enforcement
iii) an unstable international system, and
iv) a major economic crisis.

It was therefore a time of great uncertainty for everyone, and an opportunityopportunity for an ex-corporal from Austria who had a very clear vision about how he wished the future to unfold.

References.
1   W.S. Churchill, *The Second World War*, vol.1 (London, 1948), viii.
2   Fritz Fischer, *Griff nach der Weltmacht* (Düsseldorf, 1961) - published in translation as *Germany's aims in the First World War* in 1967.
3   Klaus Hildebrand, *The Foreign Policy of the Third Reich* (Batsford, 1973).
4   For a good discussion of these historians see A.Crozier, *The Causes of the Second World War* (Blackwell, 1997), pp. 229-230.
5   T.W. Mason, *Social Policy in the Third Reich* (Berg,1993), p. 265.
6   Crozier, *The Causes of the Second World War*, p. 227.
7   Alan Sharp, 'Versailles 1919: "A Tragedy of Disappointment"', in Peter Catterall and Richard Vinen, *Europe 1914-1945* (Heinemann, 1994), p. 16.
8   Anthony Lentin, 'The Consequences of the Versailles Settlement', ibid., p. 23.
9   Ruth Henig, *Versailles and After 1919-1933* (Methuen, 1984), p. 45.
10 Ibid., p. 44.

Working on Chapter I

Note-making is the foundation of all your learning - the basis for both essay writing and revision. It is also an active process that requires you to concentrate while you read. The subdivisions of this chapter make it relatively easy to decide on headings, but deciding on the level of content is not so easy. Do not write out the whole book - there is no point - but on the other hand make sure you do not miss anything important. This is not an easy task at the beginning when you are unfamiliar with a topic

This chapter is essentially introductory; but it is important you absorb the background material. It is divided into five sections.

i)   The first section deals with the historiography of the subject and iden-
     tifies a number of key questions raised by historians' investigations. It
     is essential you keep these questions in mind when you read through
     the book.
ii) The second section is an overview of the book and is subdivided a) to
     e), roughly corresponding to the chapters in the book.

The next three sections deal with the background to Hitler's coming to power, by looking at:

iii) the Paris Peace settlement
iv) the lack of consensus in the 1920s and
v)   the Great Depression.

All of these factors serve to explain why the German people were so disgruntled that they turned away from democracy in the early 1930s and why a substantial number turned to Adolf Hitler.

Summary Diagram
Introduction

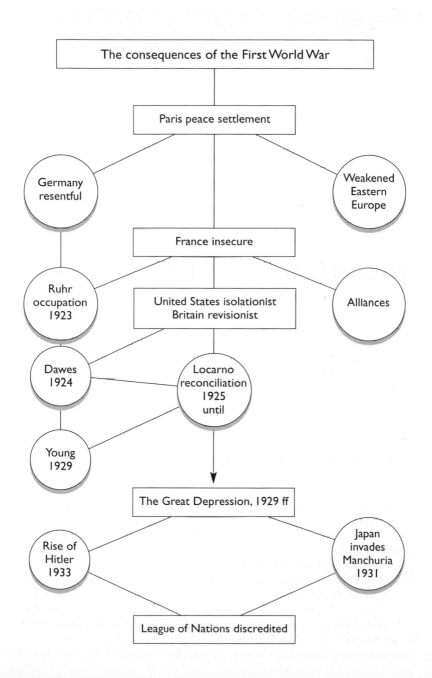

2 Hitler Comes to Power 1933-5

POINTS TO CONSIDER

This chapter will look at the origins of Hitler's thinking before going on to look at his first two years in office, culminating in the reintroduction of conscription. You may wish to consider just how cautious he was and just how his underlying ideological position affected his behaviour in this early period.

KEY DATES

1920   Hitler and Drexler draw up the Nazi 25 point programme
1924   Hitler writes *Mein Kampf*
1933   Hitler becomes Chancellor (January) and pulls out of both the Disarmament Conference and the League of Nations (October); Rapallo terminated
1934   German Non-Aggression Pact with Poland (January), Disarmament Conference ends (April), Hitler visits Mussolini (June), Mussolini orders troops to Austrian border to thwart Nazi coup (July)
1935   Saar plebiscite victory for Hitler (January), Hitler announces the existence of the Luftwaffe and the reintroduction of conscription (March), Stresa Front (April), Franco-Soviet Mutual Assistance Pact (May), Anglo-German Naval Pact (June)

1 Hitler's Ideology

> **KEY ISSUE** What were the origins of Hitler's thinking and how did it develop?

a) Early Years

Many historians contend that Hitler's belief that the Germans were a master race destined to colonise the East was fundamental to his foreign policy thinking. If you too decide that his policy was ideology-driven - that is to say, it was governed by a body of firmly-held ideas and long-term plans rather than being an improvisation based on opportunities - then the origins of his thinking are of paramount importance. However, attempts to explain them by reference to his early childhood are just speculation. For instance, the most recent attempt to link his anti-Semitism with the presence of the philosopher Wittgenstein at his school in 1904-5 - based on a single reference in his autobiographical work, *Mein Kampf* (My Struggle), to 'one Jewish boy ... we did not particularly trust' - has not impressed reviewers.[1] However, there is no doubt that Hitler's experience from 1907 in Vienna, where Jewish families were socially successful, did have an impact on his thinking. In particular, Jewish entrants were disproportionately successful at the Academy of Fine Arts, where Hitler failed to get in. Hitler's childhood friend from 1904 to 1908, August Kubizek, records that the young Adolf constantly complained about the multiethnicity of German Vienna and in particular expressed his dislike for the Jews.[2]

But racism and anti-Semitism were not unusual at that time. Anti-Semitism had a long history (going back to Jesus's condemnation by the Sanhedrin) and was particularly virulent in Austria and Germany. Indeed specifically anti-Semitic political candidates were elected to the German Reichstag, admittedly in small numbers, from the 1880s. Kaiser Wilhelm II himself told Sir Edward Grey in 1907 that 'they want stamping out' and later he was to suggest gas as a means of efficient extermination.[3] Towards the end of the nineteenth century racism in general was given a pseudo-scientific boost by Social Darwinism, the application of biological evolution to human society. Thus Jews were not only defined in terms of religion or appearance but in terms of a biologically determined inferior race. Human life, like animal life, was described as a struggle for survival, the 'survival of the fittest' as the philosopher Herbert Spencer put it, and the idea of white superiority, the superiority of the so-called (and rarely defined) Aryan race, was further developed by another British philosopher, Houston Stewart Chamberlain, whom Hitler met and admired.[4] These views gained wide currency. Indeed in 1914, many in the upper echelons of the German government saw the forthcoming war as a biological racial war, a struggle between teuton and slav, and even in the 1919 peace settlement Britain and America refused Japan's request to include a declaration of racial equality. What we have to remember, then, is that Hitler's thoughts were not unusual; he was very much a product of his own times, but at the same time we have to acknowledge that he carried these ideas to unimaginably violent extremes.

The impact of the war on Hitler was no doubt considerable, but of course it was the shock of defeat and the desire for revenge that turned him into a political animal, as he himself stated in his autobiography. Without the defeat or indeed perhaps without such a (perceived) harsh peace settlement, it is unlikely that Hitler's views would have ever developed or been important. Of perhaps equal significance was the year after the war when Hitler attended a number of army indoctrination courses and discovered his considerable ability to speak to an audience.

Indeed it is not until the post-war period that we can have any concrete evidence of Hitler's thinking. Thus, it is from 1919 onwards that we are able to build up a real picture of his thought and its later implications for foreign policy.

ADOLF HITLER (1889-1945)   **- *Profile* -**

Hitler was born in Braunau in Austria on April 20 1889. After leaving school in Linz he went to Vienna to become an artist but was unsuccessful and became a drifter. He then went to Munich and joined the German army in 1914, served in the war, and was awarded the Iron Cross First Class. After the war he joined the Nazi party and became its leader. The failure of an attempted coup (the Munich Putsch) in 1923 led to his imprisonment for nine months at which time he wrote his semi-autobiographical work *Mein Kampf* in which he expounded his views on race and space. Here he talks about Germany's need for *Lebensraum*:

1   And so we National Socialists consciously draw a line beneath the foreign policy tendency of our pre-War period. We take up where we broke off six hundred years ago. We must stop the endless German movement to the south and west, and turn our gaze
5   towards the land in the east. At long last we break off the colonial and commercial policy of our pre-War period and shift to the policy of the future. If we speak of soil in Europe, we can primarily have in mind Russia and her vassal border states.

from *Mein Kampf*, first published in 1925

The Depression brought the Nazis dramatic success in the elections of 1930 and 1932, and on January 30 1933 Hitler became Chancellor. He quickly eliminated his opponents and turned Germany into a one-party-state. His attempts to reverse Versailles and unite all Germans led to rearmament, the remilitarization of the Rhineland, *Anschluss* with Austria, the annexation of part of Czechoslovakia and an attack on Poland which precipitated the outbreak of the Second World War in September 1939. Prior to this Hitler had made clear that the next war would be a racial war:

1   Today I will once more be a prophet: if the international Jewish financiers in and outside Europe should succeed in plunging the nations once more into a world war, then the result will not be the Bolshevising of the earth and thus the victory of Jewry, but the anni-
5   hilation of the Jewish race in Europe!

from a speech to the Reichstag, January 1939

After defeating France (but not Britain) he turned on Russia in 1941. However, by 1943 this campaign had failed and with the opening up of a western front in 1944, Hitler's days were numbered. He committed suicide with his mistress Eva Braun in a bunker in Berlin on April 30 1945. During the course of the war his appalling racial theories were put into practice and over six million Jews were exterminated.

b) Sources

What are our sources up to 1933? Principally we rely on the Nazi Twenty-Five Point Programme that Hitler drew up with Anton Drexler in February 1920, his autobiographical book *Mein Kampf*, which was published in two volumes in 1925 and 1927, *Hitler's Second* or *Secret Book*, written in 1928 but not published until 1961, and his letters and his speeches, which date from 1919.[5]

It is possible to identify the evolution of Hitler's thought between the years 1919 and 1924. In 1919 his foreign policy objectives were quite conventional, similar to those of the Pan-German League. In his speech of September 1919 he spoke of a 'Greater Germany'; in that of December 1919 he stated, 'the removal of our colonies represents an irreparable loss for us'; and in the Twenty Five Point Programme of February 1920, it was stated:

1. We demand the union of all Germans in a Greater Germany on the basis of the right of national self-determination.
2. We demand equality of rights for the German people in its dealings with other nations, and the revocation of the peace treaties of Versailles and St. Germain.
3. We demand land and territory [colonies] to feed our people and to settle our surplus population.
4. Only members of the nation may be citizens of the State. Only those of German blood, whatever their creed, may be members of the nation. Accordingly no Jew may be a member of the nation.[6]

Thus Hitler wanted a revision of the Treaty of Versailles, the creation of a new Greater Germany to accommodate all 'pure' Germans including those Germans of the former Habsburg Empire - in Austria and Czechoslovakia - who had never been part of Germany, and the return of Germany's lost colonies. At this stage he saw France and Britain as the main obstacles and Italy as a potential ally. Russia was seen as a potential ally until he was convinced that all Bolsheviks were Jews. Anti-Bolshevism thus became as important as anti-Semitism. The French occupation of the Ruhr in 1923 changed his perspective some-what, as Britain opposed the operation, and he came to see her as a potential ally too. He actually admired the British not only because of their Empire but because he also felt that there was a racial affinity. However, an alliance with Britain would preclude the recovery of the colonies, and thus Hitler came to think in terms of acquiring territory elsewhere, in the East. Accordingly, by the time he wrote *Mein Kampf*, he had further developed points three and four of the Nazi programme.

Hitler was convinced that the outcome of the great racial struggle would depend upon population, territory and resources, but Germany was 'a nation without space' (the blockade had demon-strated its vulnerability). The only solution was the acquisition of living space (*lebensraum*) in the East (which to some extent echoed what happened at the treaty of Brest-Litovsk in March 1918 when Imperial Germany annexed a vast amount of Russian territory, albeit for a short time). This could only be achieved by struggle; Hitler rejected peaceful economic means to achieve these aims. As he stuck religiously to this policy and it had important implications for later foreign policy, it is worth quoting *Mein Kampf* at length:

1 Germany has an annual increase in population of nearly 900,000. The difficulty of feeding this army of new citizens must increase from year to year and ultimately end in catastrophe unless ways and means are found ... Nature knows no boundaries ... she confers the master's right on
5 her favourite child, the strongest in courage and industry ... Only a sufficiently large space on this earth can ensure the independent existence of a nation ... As members of the highest species of humanity on this earth, we have a[n] obligation ...[to] ... fulfil ...The acquisition of land and soil [must be] the objective of our foreign policy ...The demand for
10 the restoration of the frontiers of 1914 is a political absurdity ... We are ... turning our eyes towards the land in the East ... The colossal empire in the East is ripe for dissolution. And the end of the Jewish domination in Russia will also be the end of Russia as a state ... Today we are not struggling to achieve a position as a world power; we must
15 fight for the existence of our fatherland, for the unity of our nation and the daily bread of our children. If we look around for allies from this point of view, only two states remain: England and Italy.[7]

The *Second* or *Secret Book*, written just a few years later, was largely a restatement of *Mein Kampf*, though Hitler did express concern about France's alliance with Poland (1921) and Czechoslovakia (1924), and he did address Britain's policy of trying to keep a balance of power on the continent by ensuring that no single power came to dominate. This balance of power policy he believed to be incorrect, as a Greater Germany was no threat to the world-wide interests of the British Empire. However, he did point out there was no limit to the expansion of a racially superior nation.

It cannot be emphasised too often that race and space remained central to Hitler's thinking throughout - the union of all Germans, the master race, in a Greater Germany and *lebensraum* in the east; Hitler was obsessive about these fundamental concepts. He held them with a messianic fervour. How far this was a novel policy is a moot point. Expansionism had been fundamental to the 'men of 1914' in the September Programme, in Brest-Litovsk and they also saw warfare as a biological struggle between the races, between teuton and slav. However, Hitler brought these two concepts together with greater intensity and carried them to their logical and appalling conclusion.

Hitler returned to the same theme in speech after speech between 1928 and 1933, but naturally when he came into office in 1933 he stopped making reference to these ideas in public. Yet in private, as we shall see, he constantly returned to them - in briefings, in letters, in his *Table Talk* during the war and finally in his *Political Testament*. Indeed the consistency of Hitler's views both before and after coming to power is really quite striking.

Of course not all historians subscribe to the primacy of ideology as the determinant of Hitler's foreign policy. Some see him as more of an opportunist and point out the contradictions in his actions, but we will consider this alternative view later (see page 56). For the time being it is essential that you at least keep the question in the back of your mind - was Hitler's foreign policy ideology-driven? If you accept that it was, then it is clear that German expansion meant war. However, dreams of conquest and empire are one thing, reality is another. How was Hitler going to achieve such fantastic objectives?

2 The First Two Years, January 1933-January 1935

> **KEY ISSUE** What did Hitler achieve in his first two years in office?

a) The First Year

It is important to remember that when Hitler became Chancellor in January 1933 he did not have full control over the government (he was in a coalition), over the army (the soldiers owed allegiance to President Hindenburg) or even over his own party (Röhm and the S.A., the brownshirted Nazi stormtroopers used to enforce 'discipline', were by no means his poodles). Accordingly, he had to proceed with caution. It would therefore be some years before he could really take the initiative with regard to international affairs. In any event, in this matter he stepped on to a moving conveyer-belt, as it were, with events already in train (see Chapter 1), and although he had long-term objectives, he had no detailed plan - indeed no real idea how he was going to achieve them. However, such 'structural' factors did not determine the direction of foreign policy; Hitler's intentions did.

Throughout 1933 and 1934 (see table overleaf) he took steps to consolidate his position within Germany, assuming dictatorial powers, banning other parties, eliminating Röhm and his cronies (as much to please the army as himself) and, after the death of Hindenburg, assuming the presidency (and the title of Führer) to which the army owed an oath of loyalty (August 1934). In private, Hitler continued to express his true objectives. As early as 3rd February 1933 he told the generals that Versailles had to be overthrown, that rearmament was the most pressing priority, that 'National Service[i.e. conscription] must be reintroduced' and that once Germany was sufficiently powerful, the regime would achieve 'the conquest of new living space in the East and its ruthless Germanisation'.[8]

Timeline of Hitler's Consolidation of Power

1933

30 Jan	Hitler becomes Chancellor
27 Feb	Reichstag fire
28 Feb	Hitler given emergency powers
3 March	Communists arrested
23 March	Enabling Act gives Hitler 4 years' dictatorial power
31 March	Local government brought under Nazi control
2 May	Trades Unions banned
14 July	Germany officially becomes a one-party state
30 Nov	Gestapo created

1934

30 June	'Night of the Long Knives' - S.A. purged
2 Aug	President Hindenburg dies
	Hitler becomes President
	Army swears oath of allegiance to him
19 Aug	Hitler proclaims himself Führer and Reich Chancellor

In public Hitler protested his desire for peace in a series of speeches and interviews throughout 1933, stating 'nobody wishes for peace more than I'. These utterances were of course designed to camouflage the Nazi consolidation of power and an acceleration in rearmament. In fact the whole question of armaments was currently centre stage at the Disarmament Conference in Geneva. Prior to Hitler the Foreign Ministry had already taken a hard line on this issue, requesting parity of armaments; now in October 1933, using France's refusal to entertain this point, Hitler pulled out of both the Conference and the League of Nations and cleverly held a confirmatory plebiscite (a vote to approve what he had done) in November, achieving 95 per cent approval.

What helped Hitler at this time was a growing change in attitude in Britain. By the 1930s a new historical climate was emerging which suggested that perhaps Germany had not been solely responsible for the outbreak of the First World War after all; accordingly the British government was quite prepared to allow some German rearmament, which it knew was already secretly under way, provided it was the result of negotiation and agreement. In order to get Germany back into the conference, Britain proposed an increase in the German army (to 200,000), a reduction in the French army (from 500,000 to 200,000), and agreed that Germany should have an air force half the size of the French. Indeed Britain spent six months trying to get Germany back into the talks and this gave Hitler excellent cover for the first risky stages of rearmament. No one wished to torpedo the Conference by denouncing Germany, but France finally blew the whistle in April 1934 by pointing out that the German budget was clearly designed for rearmament. This finally brought the Disarmament Conference to an end. In the meantime Hitler attempted to make bilateral agreements, starting with Britain, suggesting Germany would guarantee the British Empire in return for a free hand in Eastern Europe and proposing a Non-Aggression Pact and a naval Agreement (November 1933), but Britain would not be drawn at this stage.

b) The Second Year

Much to everyone's surprise, on 26 January 1934, Hitler concluded a Non-Aggression Pact with Poland against the wishes of the Foreign Ministry. Although the initiative to some extent came from the Poles, Hitler had good reasons for concluding this agreement - it was designed to upset the French (who had an alliance with the Poles) and reflected his wish to move away from Russia. The Rapallo treaty, which had originally been signed between the Weimar Republic and the Soviet Union in 1922 (see page 11), had been terminated at the end of 1933 and Soviet overtures in March 1934 were rebuffed (for a full discussion of Soviet foreign policy, see Chapter 6.2). As the Polish Pact also risked his popularity, in view of the German dislike of Polish 'occupation' of German territory (the Polish corridor cutting off East Prussia - see the map on page 8), many foreign observers regarded it as an act of statesmanship. Of course we know, with hindsight, that it was merely a cynical ploy to buy time. Hitler said privately at the time, 'I have no intention of maintaining a serious friendship with Poland'.[9]

In June 1934 Hitler visited Mussolini to cultivate his friendship but the meeting was not a success; *Il Duce* ('the leader', as Mussolini was known) was not impressed. Moreover, the following month, when the Austrian Nazis assassinated Chancellor Dollfuss and attempted a coup, Mussolini ordered troops to the Austrian border to indicate his opposition to any such action. Relations with Germany became tense. Although the Austrian Nazis had probably acted on their own initiative, it should be remembered that Hitler, an Austrian by birth, was committed to *Anschluss* in the long term. This was a dangerous time for the German leader, but as we shall see (page 25) the democracies were insufficiently united to devise a coordinated policy with Italy against Germany. Although in September, Russia joined the League of Nations and Britain and France issued a guarantee of Austrian independence, there was no attempt to take any concrete steps against Hitler.

In the last months of 1934, Hitler concentrated on the preparations for the plebiscite in the Saar, which was held by the League of Nations in accordance with the terms of the Treaty of Versailles. In 1919 the Saarland had been, in effect, placed under French control for

15 years and now the people were being offered the chance of returning to the Reich. The plebiscite was held in January 1935 and resulted in an overwhelming vote (90.9 per cent) in favour of return. This was a triumph for Hitler. Thus he had survived a period of extreme vulnerability unscathed, and, at the end of two years in office, was in a much stronger position. Now he no longer felt the need to disguise his rearmament programme.

3 Rearmament and Reactions

> **KEY ISSUE** How did the western democracies respond to Hitler's blatant defiance of the Treaty of Versailles?

a) Conscription

From the very beginning Germany had ignored the rearmament clauses of the Versailles treaty, building aircraft, and training and expanding its army, usually with the cooperation of the Soviet Union. There was, therefore, considerable continuity between Weimar and Nazi policy (though not in terms of co-operation with Russia). However, Hitler dramatically increased the pace. As early as the beginning of February 1933 he informed both the generals and the cabinet that rearmament was the main priority, and of course in this policy he had the full support of the armed forces and the old conservative elite. By 1935 it was becoming impossible to disguise the growth of the armed forces. On 4 March Britain gave German armaments as a reason for new rearmament plans. A few days later the French extended the period of military service. Cleverly exploiting these moves by the democracies, Hitler then announced the existence of the German airforce, the *Luftwaffe*, and on 16 March issued a decree introducing conscription, coupled with a declaration that Germany had no further intention of observing the defence limitations of the Versailles treaty.

As early as December 1932 plans had been activated by the Weimar Republic to triple the army from 100,000 to 300,000. Thus by 1935 the army had increased from seven to 21 divisions, and conscription envisaged a further increase to 36 (over half a million men). Similarly the *Luftwaffe* grew from just a few hundred planes in 1932 to some 2,500 by 1935. However, as a proportion of the gross national product (GNP), military expenditure was still relatively low - it was not until 1936 that rearmament was really stepped up. Nevertheless, expenditure had increased from 2.7 billion marks in 1933 to 8 billion marks in 1935, enough to give Germany greater comparability with the other powers, and enough to cause other powers concern. Germany was now catching up. Indeed Hitler went out of his way to exaggerate the extent of rearmament (claiming in March 1935, for instance, that the

Luftwaffe was as large as the RAF), because he believed that a Germany which was perceived to be strong would not be attacked - not that any of the other powers planned to do this. But why was Hitler allowed to tear up the Versailles settlement so easily? The lack of any coordinated response from the other powers needs to be explained.

b) The Response of the Democracies

The envoys of Britain and France in Berlin had no illusions about Hitler. André François-Poncet warned Paris that the new Chancellor was a man of action rather than words, and in a series of reports Sir Horace Rumbold told London that Hitler was a serious threat to his neighbours and the peace of the world. The French took their man's impressions seriously, but Britain was not a neighbour and the government felt that Rumbold was alarmist. Whitehall felt that power would tame Hitler and make him respectable; his earlier rhetoric was not taken literally, though his desire to revise Versailles was recognised.[10]

There are several reasons why the democracies failed to stand up to Hitler. In the case of France there was widespread revulsion against war and some sympathy for the League of Nations and the concept of disarmament. Internally there were ideological conflicts and frequent changes of government that led to paralysis in policy-making. There were three changes of government in 1932, four in 1933, two in 1934 and two in 1935. Moreover the worst effects of the Depression struck France later than in other countries, so that by the mid-thirties the economy was extremely weak. In addition, French foreign policy and French military planning were totally incompatible. Military planning was entirely defensive, whereas foreign policy revolved around giving guarantees to the states of Eastern Europe (in an arrangement known as the 'Little Entente'), guarantees that were impossible to fulfil without some sort of offensive capability. The French air force was ineffectual, with no bombing capacity, and army numbers were insufficient. For these reasons, France relied increasingly on Great Britain and was unable to take an independent line in foreign affairs. France would have liked to take a tougher line against Germany but it was just not possible, because Britain would not do so(for a fuller discussion of French and British policy, see Chapter 5).

Support for disarmament, the League of Nations and pacifism was widespread in Britain too. But Britain remained primarily a maritime and imperial power. Its eyes were not fixed on the continent, and this is where Britain and France diverged. Britain avoided fixed commitments and would not tie itself to France. Its concern was principally the defence of the Empire, and its army was widely dispersed to fulfil imperial tasks. Britain had global commitments and too few resources. Thus it had to keep an eye on not only Europe, but the Mediterranean and, in particular, the Far East as well, where

Japan was active. Defence of all these areas simultaneously was beyond Britain's capability; moreover, defence expenditure was not something that could be dramatically increased without compromising people's living standards, which were only just recovering from the Depression. This, in turn, would obviously have had significant political consequences - in short, possible electoral defeat for the politicians who carried out such a policy. These latter points applied to France too. However, where Britain and France diverged quite significantly was over Germany. The British attitude was that the Versailles settlement had been unfair to Germany and needed revision. This of course played into Hitler's hands. But Britain still considered itself to be a great power, a moral leader in the world, and as such felt that it had a right, a responsibility and indeed legitimate interests which entitled it to be involved in any revision. Changes had to be managed by consensus rather than made unilaterally.

Accordingly, there was a feeling that Hitler should be, and could be, accommodated, that it would be possible to do business with him. Furthermore he was not considered a threat at this stage and, compared with Soviet Communism, was seen as very much the lesser evil.

c) Stresa and the Naval Pact

Britain and France worked hard to make the Disarmament Conference (1932-34) work. Hitler's withdrawal from both the Conference and the League presented the democracies with a dilemma. As we have already stated, France favoured a tough line but Britain did not. Anglo-French relations were not good at this time. However, by 1935 there was a growing realisation that something had to be done about Hitler. In February Britain and France pieced together a new plan that involved Germany's return to the League, a reciprocal agreement against air attack and the legitimisation of German rearmament. At the same time (as we have already noted) Britain announced new defence preparations in March. But it was the matter of the Nazi threat to Austrian independence made manifest by the assassination of Dollfuss in July 1934 that drew Britain, France and Italy together.

France and Italy had already signed the Rome Agreements in January 1935 which settled some African questions. Between 11 and 14 April Ramsay MacDonald, the British Prime Minister, and Sir John Simon, the Foreign Secretary, met with Pierre Laval, the French foreign minister, and Benito Mussolini, the Italian dictator, at Stresa to discuss German rearmament and the status of Austria. This led to a strongly-worded condemnation of Germany's actions and reaffirmed the commitment to Locarno (see page 11) and Austrian independence. Britain also induced the League in Geneva to condemn Germany. The so-called Stresa Front offered some hope for peace and could have thwarted Hitler; Sir Eric Phipps, Rumbold's successor, reported that 'Stresa made Hitler scratch his head, Geneva made him lose it', suggesting that the German leader might have been unnerved by these developments. However, he issued a secret Defence Law very soon after, on May 21st, so he does not appear to have been deterred at all. In any event, the so-called Stresa Front proved to be only a nine-day wonder and evidence of the disunity of the western powers was not long delayed. On 2nd May 1935 France and Russia concluded a treaty of mutual assistance which did not meet with much approval in either Rome or London.

Hitler promptly took advantage of British displeasure to launch a fresh initiative (though not an original proposal) on May 21st. This quickly led on 18 June to the Anglo-German Naval Pact, which restricted the German navy to 35 per cent of British strength. This undermined Versailles and the Stresa Front and dealt a considerable blow to Anglo-French cooperation since there had been no consultation with the French government. This was a good deal for Hitler because the German navy had nothing like 35 per cent of British capacity and it therefore allowed him, in theory, to triple existing levels. Once again German rearmament was given official sanction. Hitler was understandably delighted with the agreement. From the British point of view it seemed sensible to take advantage of the offer of a voluntary agreement - particularly since Japan had withdrawn from the Washington and London naval treaties the previous December. It also seemed to rule out another naval race, like the one before the First World War. Anything that took pressure off the Royal Navy was to be welcomed at this time.

So the democracies were once again out of step even before the Abyssinian episode (see page 33) dealt the death-blow to any attempt to present a united front to Hitler. Thereafter the initiative passed to the dictators.

4 Conclusion

> **KEY ISSUE** How much of Hitler's foreign policy was continuity and how much of it was of his own making?

You now have to make a judgment about Hitler's early foreign policy. You might decide that it did not reveal anything unusual; for instance, it did not reveal his ideological aims. Indeed you might identify remarkable continuity with the policy of the previous Weimar Republic. Moreover Nazi policy at this stage reflected the wishes of the armed forces, the foreign ministry and all revisionists. It was not controversial. So, if there was nothing out of the ordinary in Hitler's policy, was his approach in some way different? Here you might be able to identify a change. If we talk about Hitler proceeding with caution in these years, as most historians do, then it should be appreciated that this caution was only relative to what came later. What often characterised Hitler's behaviour were considerable boldness and an ability to take opportunities that others might not have dared to take - what has been described as the gambler's instinct but might more reasonably be explained by reference to Hitler's self belief, his strength of will, his unshakeable certainty 'that the future would bring the fulfilment of his own world philosophy'.[11] He was clearly a man with aims who was not prepared just to react to events, as the democracies seem to have done.

In a very short space of time he had left the Disarmament Conference and the League of Nations, broken off relations with the Russians, encouraged the Austrian Nazis (though not in the assassination of Dollfuss), accelerated the pace of rearmament, reintroduced conscription, and denounced the Versailles armament limitations. Not exactly the moves of a moderate.

But if Hitler had shown great boldness, he had also shown great skill and had enjoyed not a little luck. After all, the success he enjoyed when he left the League and Conference (blaming the French) was, to some extent, lost when the Austrian Chancellor was assassinated, albeit on local initiative and not on orders from Berlin. However, the initiative was restored quite by coincidence, by the Saar plebiscite. The area was Catholic and industrial and therefore not a haven of traditional Nazi support - and the vote was free. Therefore the overwhelming pro-German result was a much needed boost for Hitler's prestige at home and abroad. Hitler was also clever in his use of propaganda, especially when he reintroduced conscription in 1935. In this matter he was able to cite British and French rearmament plans as the main reason. He seems to have been able to take a bold move and get away with it. All this led to a feeling of popular exhilaration in Germany and fed his growing self-confidence.

Of course you might identify another advantage that Hitler had, and that was his amoral position. He was prepared to say or do anything to get his own way. Thus he always tried to defuse potentially dangerous situations by saying all the things that peaceful people wanted to hear. He always coupled a bold move with some offer of peace. In addition, he made the non-aggression pact with the Poles against the advice of his foreign office because it meant nothing to him, and he offered a naval agreement to Britain just at the right moment, despite the opposition of the Navy, because the quotas also meant nothing to him. He seemed to be a good judge of his opponents, realising that they would leap at bilateral agreements even though concert diplomacy - a general agreement of all the major powers - was their aim.

The point is that for Hitler treaties were simply a means to an end, to be signed and then discarded as circumstances dictated. Hitler was able to adopt this approach because he did have ends - concrete goals, as we have indicated in the early part of this chapter. And so you might conclude that although Hitler's ideology was not revealed in his early foreign policy, it was nevertheless its driving force. That is to say, policy was driven by Hitler's messianic self-belief that Providence (his term) had placed him on this earth to destroy Versailles, unite all Germans and create a Greater German Empire in the east. But we must not make out that Hitler was cleverer than he really was; he was in fact operating in a most favourable international climate.

As we have indicated, France was weak, both politically and economically and relied on Britain to maintain the status quo. Britain, like France, was pacific but prepared to make some modifications to the Versailles treaty. Britain was also not in a strong position as it had too many commitments and too few resources and was, in any case, largely preoccupied with its imperial responsibilities. At the same time Stalin's main concern was to avoid war at all costs: the Soviet Union had just embarked on a series of five-year plans in order to catch up with the other powers. Italy enjoyed a diplomatic position of some importance that far exceeded its actual power. This was mainly due to the blusterings of *Il Duce*, Mussolini. However, Italy too was a revisionist, expansionist power and Mussolini was eager to build up the Italian Empire, in the Balkans and particularly in Africa. Japan had already shown with its invasion of Manchuria in 1931 that the League of Nations could be ignored and Britain was particularly worried about Japanese expansionism - as indeed was the United States. However, the world's most powerful nation was concerned not to be drawn into an active foreign policy at this time. The omens for Hitler were therefore good. Britain was pacific and amenable, France weak, Russia preoccupied, Italy dissatisfied and the USA in virtual isolation. Moreover within Germany Hitler had considerable support. As we have stated, although Hitler's approach to foreign policy was very much of his own making, clearly the army and industrialists were very much in favour of rearmament, the Foreign Ministry wished for the overthrow of Versailles and the mass of German people longed for the restoration of German prestige. There was therefore a considerable identity of interest that gave Hitler the green light to deal with the unfinished business of the First World War. Given Hitler's personality, this domestic climate, and his ideological aims, the pressure for continued initiatives could only gather momentum.

References

1   Richard J. Evans described *The Jew of Linz* by Kimberley Cornish as 'a ludicrous and wholly implausible mishmash of supposition and innuendo', *Sunday Telegraph*, 22 March 1998.
2   *Young Hitler* by August Kubizek (Wingate, 1954), pp. 185-7.
3   See especially John C.G. Röhl, *The Kaiser and his Court* (CUP, 1990), Chapter 8.
4   See also R. Pearce, *Fascism and Nazism* (Hodder, 1997), pp. 18-21.

5   See J. Noakes and G. Pridham *Nazism, A Documentary Reader* vol 3 (Exeter
    U. P., 1988), pp. 609-623 - hereafter Noakes and Pridham, *Nazism.*
6   Ibid, vol 1, p.14.
7   Ibid, vol 3, pp. 614-616.
8   Ibid, p. 629.
9   Quoted in G. Craig, *Germany 1866-1945* (OUP, 1978), p.681.
10 Ibid, pp. 674-5.
11 I. Kershaw, *Hitler* (Longman, 1991), p. 118.

Source-based questions on 'Hitler's Ideology'

Read the extracts from the Nazi Programme and *Mein Kampf* quoted
on pages 19 and 20 and answer the following questions:
a) Why did point two of the Programme refer to the Treaty of St.
   Germain (line 5)? (3 marks)
b) What was the thinking behind point four of the Programme and references to 'members of the highest species of humanity' in *Mein Kampf*
   (line 00)? (3 marks)
c) What is the 'colossal empire in the East' that Hitler was referring to
   and why was it 'ripe for dissolution'(lines 11 and 12)? (3 marks)
d) In what ways does the extract from *Mein Kampf* differ from, or go
   beyond, the extract from the party programme, and what brought
   about these changes? (6 marks)
e) Using your own knowledge as well as the texts, would you agree that
   the documents are reliable sources for Hitler's thinking? (10 marks)

Hints and Advice
Documentary exercises at AS and A level usually test your understanding of extracts from contemporary sources and/or historians.
The objective in a series of questions is usually to test recall (i.e.
memory/knowledge), comprehension (your understanding of a
source), and comparison and evaluation (how reliable or useful
sources are in themselves or in relation to each other). An overall
assessment would usually require you to combine an evaluation of all
the sources with your knowledge, in answer to a specific question.

Questions a), b), and c) are designed to test your knowlege and
comprehension of Hitler's background and ideology, whereas d)
requires you to compare the content of two sources and explain the
differences - again by means of your knowledge of how Hitler's
thinking evolved. Question e) is an overall assessment as described
above, and requires you to have a broad knowledge of Hitler's
thinking throughout this lifetime. These particular questions, then,
are largely a test of knowledge since the sources in themselves are
uncontroversial and do not need to be assessed for deception or bias.

Structured Question on 'Hitler Comes to Power 1933-5'

a) Explain why Hitler disliked the Jews. (4 marks)
b) Outline why he introduced conscription. (6 marks)
c) To what extent was Hitler operating in favourable circumstances? (10 marks)

Hints and advice
With structured questions you must be careful to tailor the length of your answer to the marks available. It is a common mistake for students to write at length for a question that is worth, say, 4 marks and then to write less for one which is worth 10. Writing at length in answer to the early low mark questions also leaves you little time to complete the entire exercise.

When a question offers 4 marks or 6 marks that does not usually mean that the examiners are looking for four or six points; sometimes they are looking for two or three points and you obtain the extra marks by developing your answer. Thus in the case of a) your two points might be that Hitler's anti-semitism was on the one hand a product of his exposure to contemporary beliefs; and on the other a product of his personal experience in Vienna. To develop these two points you might point out that anti-semitism had recently developed a pseudo-scientific dimension based on the racial biology of Social Darwinism and this undoubtedly influenced Hitler. As far as his personal experience is concerned, you would point to the success of Jews in Vienna, in particular at the Art Academy where Hitler was rejected.

As far as b) is concerned your three points might be his wish to overturn Versailles, his wish to consolidate his regime, and his long-term plans. To double your marks you would develop each point by referring to the military clauses of Versailles, by pointing out that conscription pleased the army and reduced unemployment and finally by looking at his goals for a racial union of all Germans and expansion in the East - for which he undoubtedly needed a large army.

Question c) requires you to refer back to Chapter 1 - the unstable international system and the effects of economic depression as well as the reactions of specific countries. Remember, answers to structured questions have to be relevant and you have limited time. Be concise and answer the question directly.

Summary Diagram
Hitler Comes to Power, 1933-5

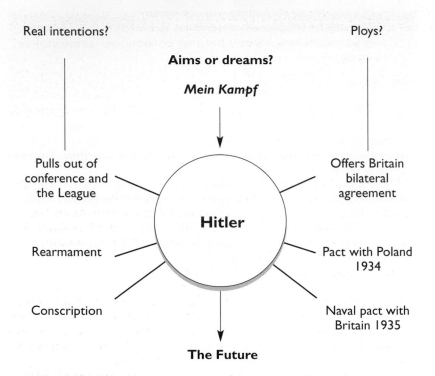

3 The Diplomatic Revolution 1935-7

POINTS TO CONSIDER

This chapter will take you through the Abyssinian episode which led to Italy and the democracies falling out, enabled Hitler to reoccupy the Rhineland and ultimately led to the Rome-Berlin Axis. You need to consider how important these developments were in helping Hitler to fulfil his goals.

KEY DATES

1934   Wal-Wal incident (December)
1935   Invasion of Abyssinia (October); Hoare-Laval Plan (December)
1936   Hitler moves troops into Rhineland (March); Addis Ababa falls (May); outbreak of Spanish Civil War (July); Hitler introduces Four Year Plan (September); Rome-Berlin Axis (Oct/Nov); Anti-Comintern Pact (November)
1937   Mussolini visits Hitler (September)

What enabled Hitler to pursue his aims with greater confidence and flexibility was the diplomatic revolution that occurred in these years. The main cause of this change was the Italian dictator, Benito Mussolini whose actions over Abyssinia (today Ethiopia) led to a split with the democracies and reconciliation with Germany.

Benito Mussolini - the man who took the lid off

1 The Invasion of Abyssinia 1935

> **KEY ISSUE** Why did Mussolini invade Abyssinia and why was Anglo-French policy so indecisive?

The Italian state had long coveted Abyssinia but had been humiliated by defeat at Adowa in 1896. Nevertheless, in 1906 Britain and France had recognised the area as an Italian sphere of influence. However, Italy gained little in the 'mutilated' peace of 1919 and her frustrated colonial ambitions soured relations with the democracies in the post-war period. Italy tried to win over Abyssinia by friendship in the 1920s, sponsoring her membership of the League of Nations in 1924 against British and French objections, and signing a treaty of friendship in 1928. However, this policy was unsuccessful and by the 1930s Mussolini was getting impatient. The possibility of an invasion had been discussed as early as 1925 but actual plans were not drawn up until 1932.

Mussolini wished to conquer Abyssinia to avenge 1896, but primarily for reasons of prestige. It was also hoped that the colony would be an outlet for Italian colonists, a source of recruits for the army and of economic value, but imperial aggrandisement was the fundamental motive. Mussolini was obsessed with the idea of reconstituting the Roman Empire - albeit in a place where the Caesars had never been. And the timing had a lot to do with Hitler's coming to power. A powerful Germany was seen as a threat initially, and Mussolini felt he had to move before Hitler tried for Austria again.

Italy was not a strong power: she lacked basic industrial raw materials like coal and iron. That she enjoyed a position of some diplomatic stature was largely due to the efforts of Mussolini, who exaggerated Italy's capabilities at every opportunity, and Hitler's coming to power, which unnerved the democracies. Accordingly by the 1930s France was contemplating giving Italy a free hand in Abyssinia. However, although it had been perfectly acceptable to carve Africa up prior to 1914, in the post-war world new rules applied. Some might say that this was because Britain and France had already acquired what they wanted and were therefore prepared to pay lip-service to America's anti-colonial stance. Moreover Italy had mistakenly made Abyssinia a member of the League of Nations, with all the rights that go with membership.

Still, in January 1935 Pierre Laval, the French foreign minister, visited Rome and Mussolini later claimed he had offered Italy a free hand in Abyssinia. Whatever was intended - and French policy was certainly ambiguous - Mussolini took it as a green light. The Stresa agreement (see page 26) boosted *Il Duce's* confidence, and in June France and Italy signed a secret treaty to guarantee Austrian independence. Britain, on the other hand, was categorically not prepared to

BENITO MUSSOLINI (1883-1945) — *Profile* -

Mussolini was born in Predappio in the Romagna. He became a member of the Socialist Party and edited its newspaper *Avanti*. He served in the war and split with the Socialists over this issue. After the war in 1919 he founded the Fascist movement and became violently anti-socialist. He came to power in 1922 and gradually established himself as the dictator of a one-party-state. As he stated:

> This is our formula: all within the state, nothing outside the state, nothing against the state ... What occurred in October 1922 was not a change of Ministry, it was the creation of a new political regime.
>
> from a speech of October 1925

His aim was to make Italy 'great, respected and feared' as he put it, and every Italian was to become a good Fascist:

1 The whole country has to become a great school for perpetual
  political education which will make Italians into complete Fascists,
  new men changing their habits, their way of life, their mentality;
  their character and finally, their physical make-up. It will no longer
5 be a question of grumbling against the sceptical, mandolin-playing
  Italians, but rather of creating a new kind of man who is tough
  strong-willed, a fighter; a latter-day legionary of Caesar for whom
  nothing is impossible.

> from a conversation in 1931

This theme of a link with the ancient Roman Empire was made manifest in Mussolini's expansionist foreign policy, with the take-over of Abyssinia (1935) and Albania (1939). He formed the Axis with Germany (1936) and aided Franco's Spain. At the most favourable moment (1940) he entered World War Two, but met with disaster everywhere; he was no Caesar and his soldiers were not heirs to the Roman legionaries. Although he had been popular at the time of the Lateran Accords with the Pope (1929), Abyssinia and Munich (1938), he was discarded by the Italian people in 1943. He was rescued by the Germans and ruled a puppet republic in the north of Italy, but as the allies closed in he was shot by Italian partisans on 28 April 1945 when trying to flee.

offer Mussolini a free hand - the League of Nations and the concept of collective security were very popular with the British electorate - but the government did want to remain on good terms with the Italian dictator and said nothing about the matter at Stresa. Mussolini himself intercepted an internal Foreign Office assessment which stated that Britain had no vital interests in Abyssinia. This, however, was not the same as sanctioning an invasion.

In any event, Mussolini decided to invade. Already in December 1934 an incident at Wal-Wal in which a number of Italian soldiers were killed had been used to justify retaliation and throughout 1935 military preparations went ahead. Then on 2nd October 1935 Mussolini gave a speech in which he stated:

1 When in 1915 Italy exposed itself to the risks of war and joined its destiny with that of the Allies, how much praise there was for our courage and how many promises were made! But after the common victory to which Italy had made the supreme contribution of 670,000
5 dead, 400,000 mutilated, and a million wounded, around the hateful peace table Italy received but a few crumbs from the rich colonial booty gathered by others.

  We have been patient for thirteen years, during which the circle of selfishness that strangles our vitality has become even tighter. With
10 Abyssinia we have been patient for forty years! It is time to say enough![1]

The next day Italy invaded Abyssinia. The actual campaign does not concern us here, but suffice it to say the use of airplanes and poisoned gas on poorly armed tribesmen together with nearly half a million soldiers eventually enabled Italy to prevail. Even so Addis Ababa was not taken until May 1936 and it took a further three years of considerable brutality to subdue the entire population. The cost of the campaign was enormous, Abyssinia proved to be an economic millstone and Italy was thereby seriously weakened thereafter. The most significant consequences, however, were the diplomatic ones.

It was an election year in Britain and therefore the government was quick to take the initiative in imposing League sanctions on Italy; France reluctantly followed. The sanctions were half-hearted - oil was excluded and the Suez Canal remained open - but sufficient to cause some difficulty to the Italian economy and considerable irritation to Mussolini. This was the public policy; in private a negotiated settlement was attempted. Britain wanted a League policy to please the electorate, but also wanted to avoid a breach with Italy. The result was disastrous as neither policy was pursued to a successful conclusion, as *Punch* magazine sarcastically pointed out.

In private Britain and France attempted a compromise scheme, the Hoare-Laval Plan of 8 December 1935, which proposed giving two-thirds of Abyssinia to Italy. However, the plan was leaked and the resulting furore caused it to be scrapped. In any event Mussolini would have settled for nothing less than the whole of Abyssinia. His success in this matter - in conquering the African colony, in defying the League and in effect outmanoeuvring Britain - made him enormously popular at home. This proved to be the peak of his success. He now came to despise the democracies for what he felt was their weak and spineless behaviour. Already in 1935 Mussolini had contemplated closer relations with Germany; in 1936 he realised 'only a revanchist [revengeful] Germany would back the Italian challenge to Anglo-French hegemony in the Mediterranean and help Italy become a Great Power'.[2] Italo-German relations now underwent a rapid improvement, to such an extent that Hitler was able to use the Abyssinian crisis as a cover to carry out the remilitarisation of the Rhineland a year in advance of his intentions.

Thus Abyssinia proved to be a significant turning point in European affairs. If Manchuria had begun the decline of the League, Abyssinia brought about its eclipse (all subsequent crises were handled outside the League structure); Germany had at last come out of isolation; and the democracies were in disarray. All this worked in Hitler's favour. To the Rhineland we now turn.

The awful warning - *Punch* cartoon

that Mussolini, who was keeping his options open, was to some extent playing a double game. However, conversations with London were discouraging (Britain wanted a European rather than a bilateral agreement) and Germany made a point of supplying Italy during the Abyssinian crisis despite the League ban (though Hitler's main concern was to keep the war in Africa going rather than bring it to a swift conclusion). The event which further accelerated the Italo-German rapprochement was the outbreak of the Spanish Civil war in July 1936. The nationalist leader,General Franco, appealed to both dictators; and both dictators decided to assist.

Hitler had a number of reasons for intervening: he had an eye on Spain's valuable raw materials, he wished to test out his air force, he wanted a pro-German government, he saw an opportunity to get closer to Italy, and he could portray intervention as an anti-communist crusade. Ultimately Hitler committed about 600 aircraft to the conflict; Mussolini on the other hand sent in a total of 73,000 troops, at great expense. He had been reluctant to get involved at first but eventually saw involvement as a matter of prestige. Intervention was rationalised as a move against France, and as strengthening Italy's strategic position in the Mediterranean; but in truth Italy got very little in return. Still, the Spanish Civil War polarised opinion in Europe, confirmed the democracies' weakness in the eyes of those who believed this to be the case (they adopted a policy of non-intervention), and welded Germany and Italy closer together.

In September 1936 Mussolini was invited to Germany. He accepted but sent Ciano in October to prepare the way. Hitler went out of his way to welcome Ciano and the two men signed a series of secret protocols which outlined their mutual interests. On November 1st Mussolini made a speech in Milan which coined the phrase 'Rome-Berlin Axis':

> 1 One great country has recently gathered a vast amount of sympathy among the Italian people; I speak of Germany. The meeting at Berlin resulted in an agreement between the two countries on certain questions ... But these agreements which have been included in special
> 5 statements and signed - this vertical line between Rome and Berlin is not a partition, but rather an axis around which all the European states animated by the will to collaboration and peace can also collaborate. Germany, although surrounded and solicited, did not adhere to sanctions. With the agreement of 11 July there disappeared any element of
> 10 dissension between Berlin and Rome, and I may remind you that even before the Berlin meeting Germany had practically recognized the Empire of Rome.[4]

However, the Germans were still not convinced by Ciano's assurance that Italy had abandoned all intrigue and was no longer 'the whore of the democracies'. What strengthened the tie in the end was the personal relationship that developed between Hitler and Mussolini; but that was in the future. In the meantime Hitler turned his attentions elsewhere. He still courted Britain but by sending Joachim von Ribbentrop as ambassador to London he made a grave mistake - Ribbentrop was considered a bit of a buffoon - though a bilateral agreement was never on the cards. Hitler came to see that he was better off with a newly won-over Italy. And Italian ambitions conveniently troubled the French.

Ribbentrop's most important contribution at this stage was an agreement with Japan, the Anti-Comintern Pact, which was signed in November 1936. On the surface this seemed nothing more than a propaganda ploy against communism but the agreement did hold out the prospect of closer co-operation in the future.

In general, German policy after March 1936 gradually became more strident. Clearly the Abyssinian crisis had improved her diplomatic position, but it was also the case that German military strength was increasing. In August 1936 military service was extended to a period of two years and the following month, at the Nuremburg Rally, Hitler introduced the Four Year Plan.

4 The Four-Year-Plan

> **KEY ISSUE** What can be learnt about Hitler's intentions from this plan?

The revitalisation of the German economy was essential for rapid rearmament, which in turn would enable Hitler to carry out his foreign policy. However, the German economy was still in serious difficulties in 1933 and rearmament had to be relatively modest in the first three years. It seems clear that when he was appointed Chancellor in January 1933, Hitler had no very clear idea about the kind of economic policy he would follow. However, one of his most important early decisions was to appoint Dr. Hjalmar Schacht as President of the Reichsbank, and later in 1934 as Minister of Finance, to solve the balance of payments problem.

Schacht was, above all, a brilliant financier and he now devoted his considerable gifts to the economic consolidation of the Nazi regime and, in particular, to facilitating the start of the rearmament programme. He did this by deficit financing and kept it secret by so-called 'mefo-bills', which were a type of government bond. During 1934-6 mefo-bills accounted for 50 per cent of arms expenditure (thereafter as the economy recovered, and the need for secrecy decreased, it became possible to finance rearmament from government loans and taxation). However, rapid rearmament was not possible and the little that did occur created a serious balance of payments problem as it sucked in imports of raw materials; at the same time Germany also had to import foodstuffs as her agriculture only met about 80 per cent of the country's needs - hence the difficult choice between 'guns and butter'. By early 1936 the armaments industry was only operating at 70 per cent of capacity because Germany could not afford the raw materials required. Rearmament had not exactly stalled, but it was not on course. And yet by late 1936 the economy had largely recovered. Hitler therefore decided to bring the economy more closely under party control. Some time in August 1936 he composed a memorandum launching the Four-Year-Plan - a plan to make Germany ready to wage war. In this document he talked of the forthcoming struggle with Bolshevism and Jewry and the need to develop the economy to be ready to face the danger - in particular the need to develop synthetic raw materials and become self-sufficient. He finished by stating:

1   Nearly four precious years have gone by. There is no doubt that by now we could have been completely independent of foreign countries in the spheres of fuel supplies, rubber supplies, and partly also iron ore supplies ... There has been enough time in four years to find out what
5   we cannot do. Now we have to carry out what we can do.
    I thus set the following tasks:
       i. The German armed forces must be operational within four years.
       ii. The German economy must be fit for war within four years.[5]

This last point would imply a readiness for war by 1940, but by simply looking at armaments expenditure it is hard to determine exactly what kind of war Hitler had in mind. On 4 September 1936 Herman Göring, the Commander-in-chief of the *Luftwaffe*, read out Hitler's memorandum to the cabinet stating that he, Göring, was responsible for executing the plan. The priority the Plan had over the economy soon led to a clash with the Minister of Economics, who felt the pace of rearmament was too quick and the investment in synthetic raw materials uneconomical. In November 1937 Schacht resigned. Most observers felt that he was right and that by 1939 a serious economic crisis was just around the corner. Such disproportionate expenditure on armaments would lead to a serious imbalance in the economy.

But that crisis was in the future. On 30 January 1937, the fourth anniversary of his accession to power, Hitler addressed the Reichstag proclaiming 'the withdrawal of the German signature' from the Versailles Treaty and spoke with pride of his achievements since coming to power. He also stated that 'the time of so-called weekend surprises has been ended' (a reference to the Saturday occupation of the Rhineland) and in truth there were no 'weekend surprises' in 1937. Hitler later referred to 1937 as the 'year of awareness'[6] in the sense of his final recognition that he would have to shelve the idea of a British alliance and strengthen the Italian one.

Thus in September 1937, Mussolini finally came to Germany. To honour his guest, Hitler pulled out all the stops and put on a display of considerable spectacle. Mussolini was suitably impressed. Putting their first unfortunate meeting at Venice behind them the two men developed a relationship that endured, but as time wore on Mussolini fell into the role of the subordinate partner and fell more and more under Hitler's spell. Two months later Italy joined the Anti-Comintern pact.

1937 was also a 'year of awareness' in the sense that, by the autumn, Hitler appears to have concluded that time was not on Germany's side and that she must go on to the offensive sooner rather than later. For the problem was that, by embarking on a massive rearmament programme, Germany had started an arms race. Moreover, because of her limited resources in comparison with her rivals, it was a race she was bound to lose if it went on for any length of time (he was mainly thinking of Russia). Yet there was a 'window of opportunity' which Hitler could exploit prior to the other powers catching up. He thus came under growing pressure to act quickly, using Germany's temporary superiority to expand her resources by plundering her neighbours.

Percentage of gross national product devoted to defence		
	Germany	Britain
1933	1	3
1934	3	3
1935	7.4	3.3
1936	12.4	4.2
1937	11.8	5.6
1938	16.6	8.1
1939	23.0	21.4

Despite these misgivings German military strength had developed at a remarkable rate; by the end of 1937 Germany had become the strongest military power in Europe. The rise of Germany was matched by the decline of France. Her weakness and passivity were the result of internal problems and unstable governments, and, from her point of view, British policy. The fiasco of sanctions against Italy had lost France a friend and made her even more reliant on the British, who were themselves unreliable. The Rhineland episode 'marked both a strategic and psychological surrender by France'.[7] Meanwhile, Britain continued to pursue the illusion of a general European settlement, a renegotiation of Locarno, but this was a complete non-starter. Thus by the end of 1937 the balance of power had swung decisively away from Britain and France to Germany and Italy. Italy of course was something of a paper tiger but Germany was not; and Germany now held the initiative.

References
1   S.B. Clough and S. Salvatore, *A History of Modern Italy* (Columbia U.P., 1968), p. 491.
2   P. Morgan, *Italian Fascism* (Macmillan, 1995), p. 150.
3   P.H.M.Bell, *The Origins of the Second World War in Europe* (Longman, 1997), p. 233.
4   J. Noakes and G. Pridham, *Nazism Vol. 3* (Exeter U.P., 1988), p. 672.
5   Ibid. , Vol.2 , p. 287.
6   Quoted in Noakes and Pridham, *Nazism*, p. 657.
7   Bell, p. 252.

Source-based questions on 'The Diplomatic Revolution'

1   Low and Punch

Study the cartoons on pages 33 and 37 and answer the following questions:

a)   What is the essential point that Low is trying to make in his cartoon? (3 marks)

b)   What is the message of the second cartoon and how does it differ from the first one? (7 marks)

c)   Later Mussolini was often portrayed as something of a buffoon. Why do you think he is not portrayed in this way in these cartoons? (5 marks)

Hints and advice

Often cartoons are not meant to be funny but very serious. They can sum up a whole political point of view in one simple drawing. This is why they are so widely used in newspapers and magazines. Naturally enough the cartoonist has a point of view, a bias if you like, and this is often exaggerated, not only in the message but in the drawings too (exaggerated drawings of people are called caricatures). You have to decide what the cartoonist is getting at. What does the cartoon tell you about the topic, events or people portrayed? What does it tell you about the attitude of the artist who drew the cartoon or of the magazine/newspaper which published it?

Both the Low and the Punch cartoons are contemporary and fairly explicit in conveying their message. The Punch cartoon, however, contains a variation on the original 'jingo' music-hall song first sung in 1878, when Britain confronted Russia over the creation of a large slav state in the Balkans and forced her to back down:

We don't want to fight;
But, by jingo, if we do,
We've got the men, we've got the ships,
We've got the money too.

Clearly the parody in Punch was meant to highlight the contrast with the original, somewhat more aggressive lyrics.

2   *Abyssinia and Axis*

Read the extracts from Mussolini on pages 36 and 40 and answer the following questions:
a) What is Mussolini referring to when he states 'we have been patient for forty years' (line 10)? (2 marks)
b) What does he mean when he refers to the 'few crumbs' (line 6) of rich colonial booty? Why did Italy feel cheated? (3 marks)
c) What was the essential message of the second extract and what were the consequences? (5 marks)
d) Both extracts are from speeches. How reliable are they as sources? (5 marks)

Answering Essay Questions on 'The Diplomatic Revolution 1935-7'

Consider the following questions:
1   What were the immediate consequences of Mussolini's invasion of Abyssinia?
2   In 1934 Mussolini was ready to confront Hitler; in 1937 he made a deal with him. Why?

You should use your introduction in your essay to address the question, define its terms where necessary and in effect answer it by explaining your view. The rest of the essay should then be used to justify the position you have taken at the beginning by developing the argument with relevant factual support. Remember that the greatest enemy of the effective essay is irrelevance: hence you should be addressing the question at all times, not necessarily always explicitly but certainly implicitly. By the time you reach your conclusion you should have the marks in the bag.

In the case of essay 1 you will need to identify the effect of the Abyssinian invasion on a) Britain and France, b) the League of Nations and c) Hitler. In retrospect we can see that Mussolini's invasion was an important step on the road to war, since it led to the reconciliation of the dictators and did much to give the initiative to Hitler. In essay 2 there is scope for counter-factual speculation, since if the democracies had turned a blind eye to the Abyssinian episode perhaps the Stresa Front would have held. However, you are mainly concerned with what actually happened. Do not forget to mention the significance of the Spanish Civil War in this essay.

Structured Question on 'The Diplomatic Revolution 1935-7'

a) Explain what is meant by the term 'Diplomatic Revolution' in this chapter. (4 marks)
b) Explain why Mussolini invaded Abyssinia. (6 marks)
c) In what ways was this episode a disaster for both the democracies and the League of Nations? (10 marks)

Summary Diagram
The Diplomatic Revolution 1935-7

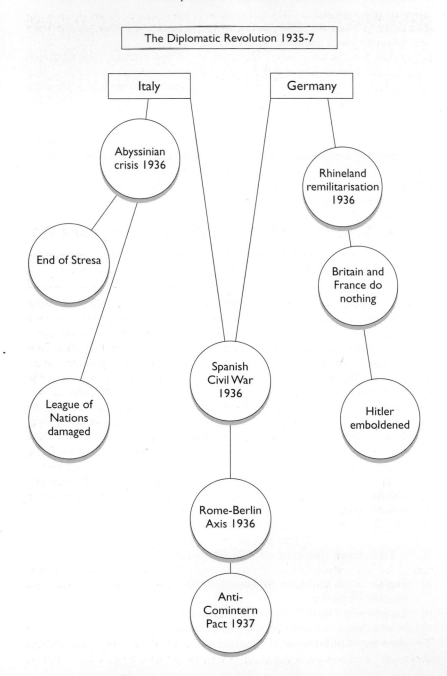

4 Hitler Changes Gear 1937-8

POINTS TO CONSIDER

This chapter will look at Hitler's planning and opportunism - the Hossbach Memorandum, his *Anschluss* with Austria, and the Munich Conference. What you have to decide is how far Hitler was in control of events and how far he was reacting to them.

KEY DATES

1937	The Hossbach Memorandum (November)
1938	The Anschluss with Austria (March); the Munich Conference (September)

1 The Hossbach Memorandum, November 1937

KEY ISSUE Can the Hossbach Memorandum be taken seriously?

As we have seen in the previous chapter, the balance of power had now shifted away from the democracies in favour of the dictators and accordingly Hitler began to take the initiative. Already in the summer of 1937, Field Marshal von Blomberg had drawn up a directive concerning 'preparations of the armed forces for a possible war' which had, among other things, discussed moves against Czechoslovakia and Austria. Then on 5 November 1937 Hitler had a four-hour meeting with five of his top brass, in which he was a little more specific about his thoughts for the future. Colonel Friedrich Hossbach, his military adjutant, took notes and five days later wrote up a secret memorandum based on the notes and his memory. This document took on some significance later at the Nuremberg trials, though all we have is a copy of a copy. Indeed it has been the subject of a great deal of historical controversy ever since. Was it a statement of intent or a mere exploration of possibilities?

Those present at the meeting
HITLER

von Fritsch	Raeder	Göring	von Blomberg	von Neurath
(army)	(navy)	(airforce)	(war minister)	(foreign minister)

Hossbach

The meeting occurred as a response to Admiral Raeder's complaints about cuts and postponements in the naval programme. The object of the meeting was to resolve the conflict over priorities in the allocation of raw materials and labour. Hitler took the opportunity to make a rambling and wide-ranging speech:

1 His exposition was to follow the fruit of thorough deliberation and the experiences of his four and a half years of power. He wished to explain to the gentlemen present the basic ideas concerning the opportunities for the development of our position in the field of foreign affairs and its
5 requirements, and he asked, in the interest of a long-term German policy, that his exposition be regarded, in the event of his death, as his last will and testament.

The Führer then continued: The aim of German policy was to make secure and to preserve the racial community and to enlarge it. It was
10 therefore a question of space.[1]

Hitler then went on to identify Germany's two main enemies, Britain and France, and he reached the conclusion that 'Germany's problem could be solved only by the use of force'.[2] He then posed three contingencies. The first was that the rearmament of the other powers meant that time was not on Germany's side; hence 'it was his unalterable determination to solve Germany's problem of space by 1943-45 at the latest'.[3] Prior to 1943-45, in contingencies two and three, Hitler felt that if France was either embroiled in internal strife or war then Germany could act sooner 'to overthrow Czechoslovakia and Austria simultaneously'.

Some historians see this document as a significant turning point in Hitler's foreign policy. Noakes and Pridham state: 'In this address Hitler had for the first time expressed a concrete commitment to war in terms of specific goals - *Anschluss* with Austria and the destruction of Czechoslovakia - and within a specific time limit - 1943-5'.[4] However, A.J.P. Taylor, in the first edition of his book, *The Origins of the Second World War*, stated that, 'Hitler's exposition was in large part daydreaming, unrelated to what followed in real life', and he further stated in 1965 that the meeting 'had no significance'.[5] Taylor attacked the source itself, pointing out that it was not a proper record, and that it was not signed by Hitler. However, others at the Conference agreed after the war that Hossbach's memorandum was a pretty reliable record of what was said. Moreover, the real significance of the meeting lay in its consequences - Hitler's remarks were taken seriously.

First of all, Operation Green (the attack on Czechoslovakia) was radically altered. At the time of the conference it was envisaged as a defensive measure because the Czechs were allied to France: it was designed to prevent a two-front war. A month later General Jodl, Chief of Operations, gave the plan a more aggressive slant:

1 When Germany has achieved complete preparedness for war in all spheres, then the military conditions will have been created for carrying

out an offensive war against Czechoslovakia, so that the solution of the
German problem of living space can be carried to a victorious conclu-
5 sion even if one or another of the Great Powers intervene against us ...
Should the political situation not develop, the execution of 'Operation
Green' from our side will have to be postponed for years. If, however, a
situation arises which, owing to Britain's aversion to a general European
War, through her lack of interest in the Central European problem and
10 because of a conflict breaking out between Italy and France in the
Mediterranean, creates the probability that Germany will face no other
opponent than Russia on Czechoslovakia's side, then 'Operation Green'
will start before the completion of Germany's full preparedness for
war.[6]

Secondly, in the ensuing discussion after Hitler's speech, both von
Blomberg and von Fritsch voiced their objections. Subsequently both
men were removed (in February 1938), but this may be mere coincidence. Hitler had not been planning major changes in the government or military - indeed he attended Blomberg's wedding in
January. However, Blomberg was made to resign when it was discovered that his new wife had been a prostitute; and von Fritsch, a single
man, was set up by Himmler and Göring and falsely accused of homo-
sexual practices. Von Neurath, who had expressed reservations after
the meeting, in January, was also removed from office at the same
time.

Blomberg's position as Minister of War was abolished and the OKW
(*Oberkommando der Wermacht* - High Command of the Armed Forces)
put in its place. Hitler absorbed the office of Commander-in-Chief of
the Armed Forces (also held by Blomberg) in addition to the post of
Supreme Commander which he already held, and he made Keitel his
Chief of Staff; von Brauchitsch, a 'yes man', replaced von Fritsch as
army commander, and von Ribbentrop replaced von Neurath at the
Foreign Office. In addition, 14 senior generals were retired, 46 others
reassigned, and new ambassadors were appointed to the key cities of
Rome, Tokyo and Vienna.

A last consequence of the meeting was that Hitler made it clear that
he had finally abandoned any thought of rapprochement with
Britain.

Of course those who criticise the document point out that the
Anschluss owed little to planning and that there was no war with
Czechoslovakia. They also point out that there is no mention of inva-
sions of Poland or Russia. All these criticisms are valid. Still, it remains
important when taken in conjunction with other evidence - for
instance, the Head of General Staff's (General Beck's) point-by-point
comments on its content written on 12 November and Jodl's revisions
of 7 December, already quoted above. It was clearly taken seriously at
the time and led to practical results. It also demonstrated beyond
doubt Hitler's warlike expansionist intentions and reflected his

growing sense of urgency (probably prompted by a bout of ill health at the time). And his comment that 'Britain, almost certainly, and probably France as well, had written off the Czechs and were reconciled to the fact that the question for Germany would be cleared up in due course', turned out to be remarkably accurate. However, as well as reflecting urgency and expansionism, the talk does suggest, by its various contingencies, that Hitler was trying to anticipate a wide variety of scenarios so that he could take advantage of the situation when any opportunity arose.

However, of more significance, perhaps, were the changes in personnel in February 1938 which made it much more likely that Hitler would be able to get his own way in the future without any objection from the army or the foreign ministry. As we have indicated, the purge of the traditional elites was in all probability an improvisation, but the Hossbach meeting did highlight their opposition. Characteristically Hitler responded 'by seizing the opportunity and, with a typically daring forward move' turned an embarrassment into a bloodless purge. 'Following the Reichstag Fire and the Röhm crisis, the Blomberg-Fritsch affair was the third great milestone on the way to Führer absolutist power'.[7] The army, the one institution of state that could still topple him, was emasculated and Hitler was increasingly surrounded by those who would simply agree with him and do his bidding. Thus his visionary intentions were able to come to replace practical, rational policy objectives. In short he was in a much better position to take the decisions he wanted to take.

2 The *Anschluss* with Austria, March 1938

> **KEY ISSUE** Did Hitler plan the *Anschluss* or was it an improvisation?

Since the abortive putsch of 1934, Hitler had been cautious towards Austria, the more so from 1936 as he did not want to jeopardise the growing friendship with Italy (see page 39). During 1937 it was Göring who increasingly took the initiative over Austria, but he envisaged *Anschluss* as evolutionary and peaceful. During Mussolini's visit in September 1937, Göring took *Il Duce's* ambiguity on the subject as a green light - a position reinforced by a report from Ribbentrop on November 6th: Mussolini had told him that he accepted that Austria was a German country. Without Italian support Austria had little chance of sustaining her independence. Moreover, she could expect little support from Britain either. When Lord Halifax visited Germany on 19 November, he stated that certain changes in Eastern Europe, notably with regard to Austria, Czechoslovakia and Danzig, 'could probably not be avoided in the long run'.[8] Accordingly, Hitler was convinced that Britain would not intervene, and when Halifax subsequently became Foreign

Secretary in February 1938, this only served to reinforce his view.

The opportunity to intervene in Austria arose early in 1938 and was precipitated by the destabilising activities of the Austrian Nazis and the Austrian Chancellor's, Schuschnigg's, exasperation with them. He came to Berchtesgaden on 12 February 1938 to discuss the matter with Hitler and there followed a remarkable meeting. Over the course of the day, Hitler ranted and raved and subjected the Austrian Chancellor to a verbal barrage of assaults, psychological pressure and threats of invasion. This was a most unusual way to conduct business between two heads of state, but it worked. Schuschnigg was forced to accept ten demands including the appointment of an Austrian Nazi, Seyss-Inquart, in the politically important post of Interior Minister (responsible for internal security with control of the police), demands that would make Austria into a virtual satellite of Germany. Indeed on 26 February Hitler said as much to some leading Austrian Nazis when he told them to drop the revolutionary approach as it was unnecessary. But then the situation changed.

The Austrian Nazis continued to hold threatening demonstrations and Seyss-Inquart increasingly came to dominate the government. Accordingly Schuschnigg tried to retrieve the situation by a desperate move: on 9 March he announced a plebiscite for 13 March on whether or not the Austrian people wanted 'a free and German, an independent and social, a Christian and united Austria'.[9] This was a bold move and it looked as though Hitler might lose - most Austrians were pro-German but ambivalent about union because it meant Nazism. Hitler was stunned. Göring effectively took charge of events and argued for military intervention, but there were no plans; however, the army quickly and willingly drew some up. In the event they were not needed as the matter was all settled on 11 March by telephone calls and telegrams. Hitler immediately wrote to Mussolini justifying German intervention and was relieved to receive a telephone call from Prince Philip of Hesse:

> *Hesse:* I have just come back from the Palazzo Venezia. The Duce accepted the whole thing in a very friendly manner. He sends you his regards.
> *Hitler:* Then please tell Mussolini I will never forget him for this.
> *Hesse:* Yes.
> *Hitler:* Never, never, never, whatever happens. As soon as the Austrian affair is settled, I shall be ready to go with him, through thick and thin, no matter what happens.
> *Hesse:* Yes, my Führer.[10]

Hitler's relief at Mussolini's acquiescence is here quite palpable. Schuschnigg, on the other hand, could get no reply from *Il Duce* - he would not pick up the phone. He could not get any joy from London either, where it was felt that *Anschluss* was inevitable and desired by the majority. France, not unusually, was paralysed by a ministerial crisis. Schuschnigg, therefore, postponed the plebiscite and resigned. On 12 March the German army marched in, but it was more of a parade than an invasion. Remarkably just as no plans had been made for the takeover, so too no plans had been laid for the actual implementation of the union - Hitler seems to have made this decision on the spur of the moment on 13 March during an emotional visit to Linz, where he had grown up. Thus Austria was annexed and became a province of the Reich, a fact which was subsequently confirmed by an all too predictable 99 per cent of the vote in a plebiscite.

The *Anschluss* with Austria was a great triumph for Hitler and enormously enhanced his personal prestige (as well as adding 295 million reichmarks to the treasury). Moreover, 'the danger of a European war arising out of the Austrian crisis was almost nil'.[11] However, the backbench Conservative MP Winston Churchill stated in the House of Commons on March 14th: 'Europe is confronted with a programme of aggression, nicely calculated and timed, unfolding stage by stage',[12] but in this case Churchill was wrong. What is important to remember about this crisis is that the date and method of *Anschluss* were forced upon Hitler by circumstances, and were *not* part of a pre-arranged plan. Hitler was compelled to improvise. But if *Anschluss* itself was not part of a plan, it was certainly another step on the road to war. The manner of the union created unease. Moreover, on 24 March 1938, Neville Chamberlain, the British Prime Minister since May 1937, warned of the dangers of a war starting in Europe. Overnight Czechoslovakia had been made more vulnerable and Hitler's self-confidence had reached new heights - Czechoslovakia would be his next objective.

3 Munich, September 1938

> **KEY ISSUE** Did Hitler get what he wanted at Munich? Was it a good deal?

Hitler despised the Czechs as 'sub-people' and possessed a personal animosity toward them that was probably the result of his contact with them in Vienna in his youth. He wished to destroy their state - but that would not be easy: the Czechs had a powerful army, a vibrant arms industry and good border fortifications. Moreover, they had a military alliance with France, prompting Hitler to describe the country as 'a French aircraft carrier in the middle of Europe'.[13] Therefore the Führer sought to undermine the state by exploiting its complex ethnic structure - in particular, by supporting the aspirations of the 3.5 million Germans who lived there (mainly in the Sudetenland - see the map on page 55). Hitler had been funding the Sudeten German Party since 1935, but there was a limit to what internal destabilisation could achieve. Czechoslovakia was an international diplomatic issue, but unbeknown to Hitler both Britain and France concluded in March 1938 that there was little they could do to assist directly in Czech defence. However, at this stage the German leader's approach was evolutionary. When on 28 March he summoned Henlein, the leader of the Sudeten Nazi Party, he simply stated that he would settle the problem in the 'not-too-distant future,'[14] but beyond that he would not be drawn. Nevertheless, Henlein was encouraged to continue his subversive tactics, negotiate demands and constantly raise them. On 24 April Henlein did just that when he presented the Czech government with his Eight Demands, which consisted of autonomy and various special rights for the German minority.

Yet a document of 20 May makes it quite clear that Hitler was in no hurry to solve the Czech problem. In an interim draft of Operation Green, Hitler told his generals:

1 It is not my intention to smash Czechoslovakia by military action in the immediate future without provocation, unless an unavoidable development of the political conditions within Czechoslovakia forces the issue, or political events in Europe create a particularly favourable oppor-
5 tunity which may perhaps never recur.[15]

Of course this was not in any way a moderate document but it certainly goes against the idea that Hitler had a strict timetable.

Ironically on the very same day a crisis erupted - the so-called May Crisis - which made Hitler change his mind completely. On May 20, acting on (unfounded) rumours of German troop movements, President Beneš of Czechoslovakia ordered a partial mobilization of the Czech army and called on the western powers to intervene. The new French government took a firm line, as did Britain: although the Czech issue was not a vital interest, the British did not wish to see a unilateral solution imposed on the Czechs by German military force. Accordingly both governments warned Hitler. Hitler made a denial (because the rumours were unfounded) but was infuriated that he had appeared to yield to Anglo-French pressure. He felt that he had been made to look foolish. Accordingly, in a fit of pique, on 28 May he summoned a meeting of leading advisers and generals and informed them: 'I am utterly determined that Czechoslovakia should disappear from the map'. He turned to the generals and stated: 'Right, we will deal with the situation in the East [i.e. Czechoslovakia] first. Then I shall give you three or four years and then we will sort things out in the West [i.e. France and Britain]'.[16] Two days later he issued a new order for Operation Green: 'It is my unalterable decision to smash Czechoslovakia by military action in the near future. It is the business of the political leadership to await or bring about the suitable moment from a political or military point of view'.[17] A covering letter from Keitel stated that the execution of the plan 'must be assured by 1 October 1938 at the latest'. So it appears that an attack of hurt pride produced the crisis, a view supported by an entry in the diary of von Weizäcker, the State Secretary in the Foreign Ministry, when he later summed up the crisis: 'His [Hitler's] resentment, stemming from 22 May when the English accused him of pulling back, led him on to the path of war'.[18] Another important consequence of this May Crisis was that the western democracies had also been disturbed by the whole incident, but their reaction was pacific. They felt that they had been taken to the brink of war and came to believe (and resent the fact) that the crisis had been manufactured by the Czechs. Neville Chamberlain, in particular, was now determined to achieve a negotiated solution to this problem which could only be favourable to Germany.

Tension mounted throughout the summer of 1938. A barrage of anti-Czech propaganda was put out by the Germans to unnerve the democracies and make them put pressure on the Czechs. German troop movements by now were quite genuine. The crisis reached a climax at the beginning of September, when on the 5th, President Beneš granted the Sudeten Germans virtual autonomy (self-rule) in an effort to defuse the situation. But Hitler wanted his war and Henlein was told to ignore this offer; Hitler used the arrest of two Sudeten deputies as an excuse to break off negotiations. He followed this up on 12 September with a violent speech at the Nuremberg Rally threatening war. This was followed by riots in the Sudetenland which now convinced Chamberlain that war was imminent. He at once resolved to take his first aeroplane journey and flew to see Hitler at Berchtesgaden on 15 September, where he agreed to Hitler's terms, subject to consultation. Hitler was none too pleased but felt that this rather ridiculous figure (as he described him) would not be back. In the meantime he contacted the Polish and Hungarian governments (which both had claims on Czech territory) and stirred up the Slovaks (who resented Czech domination).

Chamberlain obtained French acceptance for the cession of the Sudetenland to Germany on 18 September and the reluctant agreement of the Czechs on 21 September. However, when he flew back to see Hitler, this time at Bad Godesberg, he was amazed and dismayed to discover that the German leader had raised the stakes. Hitler now wanted a more rapid hand-over and a settlement of Polish and Hungarian claims. The meeting broke up with no agreement and it now looked like war.

However, a week later, assailed by last-minute doubts, Hitler pulled back from the brink. Why? There would appear to be a number of reasons. On 20 September the French began mobilisation and on the 28th the British mobilised their fleet: it was clear the democracies were now not bluffing. The Czechs too were ready to fight. In addition, Hitler's generals took fright and (rightly) maintained that Germany was not ready for a major war. Hitler also noted the lack of enthusiasm displayed by the ordinary German people and he was

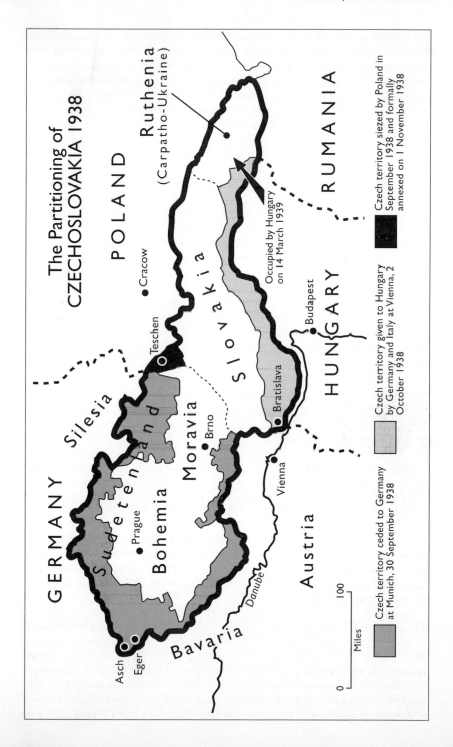

The Partitioning of
CZECHOSLOVAKIA 1938

GERMANY

POLAND

Silesia

Sudetenland

Bohemia
• Prague

Asch
Eger

Bavaria

Danube

Moravia
• Brno

Teschen

Cracow •

Ruthenia
(Carpatho-Ukraine)

Slovakia

Occupied by Hungary
on 14 March 1939

Bratislava

Vienna •

Austria

Budapest •

HUNGARY

RUMANIA

Czech territory siezed by Poland in
September 1938 and formally
annexed on 1 November 1938

Czech territory given to Hungary
by Germany and Italy at Vienna, 2
October 1938

Czech territory ceded to Germany
at Munich, 30 September 1938

0   100
Miles

influenced by Göring, who was totally opposed to war at this stage and advised caution. Moreover, the opportunity to step back from the brink was conveniently provided by Mussolini who proposed to act as a mediator at a Four Power Conference (though in truth his plan was drawn up by the German foreign office!). So, on 28 September Hitler agreed to a conference in Munich to be attended by Chamberlain, Daladier for France and Mussolini (the Czechs and the Russians were not invited - despite the fact that the former had a military alliance with the latter). There was relief throughout Europe, not least in Germany.

The meeting took place on 29 September and in the early hours of the 30th it was agreed that:

i) The Sudetenland was to be occupied by Germany between 1 and 10 October.

ii) Polish and Hungarian claims were to be settled.

iii) An international commission was to determine the final frontier.

iv) A four-power guarantee was to protect the territorial integrity of the rump Czech state.

Of greater importance to Chamberlain, however, was the subsequent Anglo-German Declaration; this was the piece of paper he proudly held up at Heston Airport on his return. It stated:

1   We, the German Führer and Chancellor and the British Prime Minister, have had a further meeting today and are agreed in recognizing that the question of Anglo-German relations is of the first importance for the two countries and for Europe.

5   We regard the agreement signed last night and the Anglo-German Naval Agreement as symbolic of the desire of our two peoples never to go to war with one another again.

We are resolved that the method of consultation shall be the method adopted to deal with any other questions that may concern our 10 two countries, and we are determined to continue our efforts to remove possible sources of difference and thus contribute to assure the peace of Europe.[19]

Chamberlain famously stated that this was 'peace for our time'. 'In reality, it was peace for a time'.[20] For Hitler it was just a piece of paper that could easily be torn up.

4 Conclusion

KEY ISSUE Was Hitler a planner or an opportunist?

Hitler felt cheated of his military victory: 'That fellow Chamberlain has spoiled my entry into Prague' he was overheard to remark.[21] And it has been rightly pointed out that 'a general war was averted in 1938 not, as is so often asserted, because Chamberlain cravenly gave way to

Hitler, but because Hitler gave way to the western powers'.[22] However, Hitler was not going to back down next time and on October 21st he issued a directive for the 'liquidation of the remainder of the Czech state'. Indeed by avoiding a war over Czechoslovakia, both Germany and the western powers probably made war more certain next time. The year 1938 had been a very good one for Hitler, but his successes were to some extent the result of fortuitous circumstances and the acquiescence of others. However, for Britain and France, Munich turned out to be the limit of concession; it was the apogee of appeasement, but it was also to be its mortal wound. Chamberlain felt that the sacrifice of the Czechs was a necessary price to pay for peace. Others were not so sure. Churchill declared: 'we have sustained a total and unmitigated defeat'.[23] Attlee, the Labour leader, concurred:

1   The events of the last few days constitute one of the greatest diplomatic defeats that this country and France have ever sustained. There can be no doubt that it is a tremendous victory for Herr Hitler. Without firing a shot, by the mere display of military force, he has achieved a domi-
5   nating position in Europe which Germany failed to win after four years of war ... He has destroyed the last fortress of democracy in eastern Europe that stood in the way of his ambition. He has opened the way for the food, the oil, and the resources that he requires in order to consolidate his military power, and he has successfully defeated and
10 reduced to impotence the forces that might have stood against the rule of violence. The cause [of the crisis] was not the existence of minorities in Czechoslovakia; it was not that the position of the Sudeten Germans had become intolerable. It was not the wonderful principle of self-deter- mination. It was because Herr Hitler had decided that the time was ripe
15 for another step forward in his design to dominate Europe ... Hitler has successfully asserted the law of the Jungle.[24]

These voices were as yet in a minority, but they were growing in number as many came to feel uncomfortable about the shabby treatment of the Czechs and giving in to Hitler. Munich did not stop Chamberlain from continuing to attempt appeasement, but for the majority it proved to be a turning point. For an analysis of appeasement in particular and the policies of the democracies in general, you are advised to turn to the next chapter, but before you do it might be worth taking another look at Hitler's successes in 1938 to see how they fit in to the debate about planning and opportunism that we referred to in the opening chapter.

As we have seen Hitler was forced to improvise when he took over Austria. There was no plan ready and precious little preparation (General Jodl reported that 70 per cent of the trucks broke down *en route!*). He was forced into *Anschluss* by Schuschnigg's threat of a plebiscite. Similarly over Czechoslovakia there were no immediate plans for a takeover; Hitler favoured the evolutionary approach but he abandoned this in May 1938 in the wake of what he felt to be a humiliation. Jodl recorded in his diary that Hitler felt 'a loss of prestige ... which he was no longer willing to take'.[25] So he planned a war. But then he did not go to war. Instead of the destruction of Czechoslovakia, he settled for a partial partition.

So, Hitler had no plan for *Anschluss* but annexed Austria, and he had a plan for a war with Czechoslovakia but he did not implement it. What does this tell us? It tells us that Hitler could improvise, be flexible, be an opportunist - it tells us he could change his mind. Does that then mean he was not a planner? The majority of historians, including his latest biographer Ian Kershaw, say no.[26] There seems to be no doubt that the absorption of both Austria and Czechoslovakia were long-term objectives of Hitler's and, as we have seen, they were referred to in the Hossbach Memorandum. After all, Hitler was only 'forced into' the take-over of Austria because taking over Austria was something that he wanted to do - otherwise he could have simply left that country alone. And his subsequent action in occupying Prague in March 1939 (see page 88) confirmed that he also wanted to expand into Czechoslovakia. So, he had objectives, but the circumstances of fulfilling them were often not of his own making.

Let us remind ourselves - at the risk of repetition - what Hitler's main objectives were: he wished to overthrow the Versailles Treaty, unite all Germans, expel all Jews and win *lebensraum* (land for German settlement) in the East (though quite why Hitler did not refer to the conquest of Russia and destruction of Bolshevism in the Hossbach Memorandum remains an unanswerable puzzle). However, within the broad framework of these long-term objectives, Hitler was prepared to improvise and be opportunistic - as indeed he was in 1938. To some extent this diagnosis of his approach was confirmed by Hitler himself in a secret speech about the previous year to a large number of senior officers on 10 February 1939 - though admittedly he wished to emphasise his forethought rather than any improvisation:

1   There was no doubt that these questions [i.e. Austria and Czechoslovakia] would have to be solved and so all these decisions were not ideas which were realised at the moment of their conception, but were long-made plans which I was determined to realise the
5   moment I thought the circumstances at the time would be favourable.[27]

It is important to remember that Hitler was an ideologue: he believed in the power of ideas, and race and space were his driving obsessions. He passionately believed in his long-term objectives and he passionately believed they were right. He also believed that he had the will to achieve them. Yet at the same time he also seems to have subscribed to a form of determinism (i.e. everything is preordained). Thus he believed that he had been chosen by Destiny or Providence (his words) to carry out these objectives and that success was assured (later when things went wrong he adopted a contrary fatalism). Now when he started to achieve success after success, this seemed to underline the determinism of his actions and he began to believe he could do no wrong - he began to speed up the process and, as we shall see, he became reckless. This increasing urgency - almost impulsiveness - that we detect in 1938 was brought about not only by the narrowing range of options imposed on him by economic restraints and other countries' rearmament (see page 43), but by his fear of an early death. In this case he feared Fate would not allow him to fulfill his great tasks - which seems to contradict the previous idea that he had been chosen. Be that as it may, historians have identified a change of habits in 1938;[28] for example, he dictated a very detailed private will (2 May 1938), he shunned physical exercise, changed his eating and drinking habits, withdrew from much conviviality and concentrated more and more on foreign policy and preparation for war - though his experience at Munich convinced him, erroneously as it turned out, that the democratic leaders would not go to war over Poland.

References

1   J. Noakes and G. Pridham, *Nazism vol. 3*, p. 681.
2   Ibid. p. 684.
3   Ibid. p. 685.
4   Ibid. p. 687.
5   Quoted by W. Simpson in *New Perspective*, September 1996, p. 34.
6   Noakes and Pridham, *Nazism*, p. 691-2.
7   Ian Kershaw, *Hitler* (Longman, 1991), p. 130.
8   Quoted in G. Craig, *Germany 1866-1945* (Oxford, 1978), p. 702.
9   P. Bell, *The Origins of the Second World War in Europe* (Longman, 1997), p. 256.
10 Noakes and Pridham, *Nazism*, p. 705.
11 Bell, *Origins*, p. 257.
12 Ibid. p. 49.
13 G. Craig, *Germany 1866-1945*, p. 702.
14 Noakes and Pridham, *Nazism*, p. 708.
15 Ibid. p. 709.
16 Ibid. p. 711.
17 Ibid.
18 Ibid. p. 720.
19 A. Crozier, *The Causes of the Second World War* (Blackwell, 1997), p. 145.
20 Ibid.
21 Noakes and Pridham, Nazism, p. 720.
22 R. Overy, *The Origins of the Second World War* (Longman, 1998), p. 29.
23 J. Lukacs, *The Hitler of History* (Vintage, 1997), p. 144.
24 Quoted in Robert Pearce, *Attlee* (Longman, 1997), p. 83.
25 Noakes and Pridham, *Nazism* Vol. 3, p. 712.
26 I. Kershaw, *Hitler 1889-1936: Hubris* (Allen Lane, 1998) appeared too late for this book, but see also his *Hitler* (Longman, 1991), p. 147 and 'Nazi Foreign Policy: Hitler's "Programme" or "Expansion without Object"?' in *The Nazi Dictatorship* (Arnold 3rd ed., 1993), pp. 108-30.

27 Noakes and Pridham, *Nazism Vol. 3*, p. 725
28 For instance J.C. Fest in *Hitler* (Pelican ed., 1977), p. 796 and J. Lukacs in *The Hitler of History* (Vintage, 1997), p. 74

Source-based questions on the 'Hitler Changes Gear 1937-8'.

1 The Hossbach Memorandum

Read the extracts from Hossbach on page 48 and Jodl's directive on pages 48-49. Answer the following questions:

a) Explain the meaning of 'racial community' in the first document (line 9) and the 'German problem of living space' (line 4) in the second document. (6 marks)

b) Why was the meeting referred to in the first document called by Hitler? (6 marks)

c) In what ways does the second document modify the plans outlined in the first? (6 marks)

d) How useful are these passages as an explanation of Hitler's policy in eastern Europe? (6 marks)

e) Why has the Hossbach Memorandum aroused such controversy amongst historians? (6 marks)

2 The Munich Settlement

Read the extracts from Chamberlain and Attlee on pages 56 and 57. Answer the following questions:

a) Explain the reference to 'the agreement signed last night' (line 5 on page 56). (5 marks)

b) Look at lines 11-16 in Attlee's speech. He does not see the crisis as being about the Sudetan Germans at all. Is he being fair? (5 marks)

c) Compare the two verdicts on the agreement. How do you explain the differences? (10 marks)

Structured Questions on 'Hitler Changes Gear 1937-8'

a) What was the *Anschluss*? (4 marks)

b) Explain why Hitler might have been disappointed with the Munich Agreement. (6 marks)

c) How justified was Hitler in claiming both Austria and Czech territory? (10 marks)

Summary Diagram
Hitler Changes Gear 1937-8

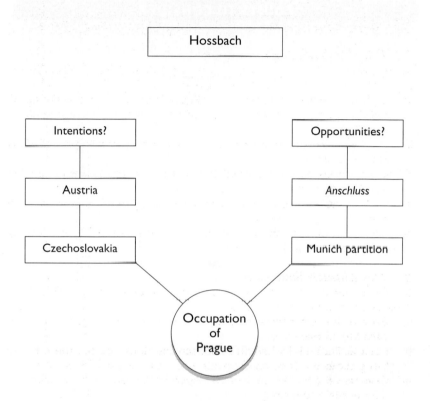

5 Appeasement

POINTS TO CONSIDER

This chapter gives you a broad overview of French and British foreign policy as well as a look at the historiography of Appeasement. You should try to appreciate the difficulties facing the democracies' policy-makers in the 1930s and then you will be better able to judge the historians' verdict.

KEY DATES

1919	Treaty of Versailles (June); Britain adopts the Ten-Year-Rule (August)
1921	Reparations fixed
1922	Washington Treaties
1923	French occupation of the Ruhr
1924	Dawes Plan
1925	Locarno Conference
1929	Maginot Line begun; Young Plan (August); Wall Street Crash (October)
1930	Allied troops evacuate Rhineland
1931	Japan invades Manchuria
1932	Ten-Year-Rule ended
1933	Defence Requirements Committee set up in Britain
1934	British rearmament begins
1935	Stresa Front (March); Franco-Soviet Pact (June); Anglo-German Naval Agreement (June); Mussolini invades Abyssinia (October)
1936	Hitler occupies Rhineland (March); Spanish Civil War breaks out (July); Popular Front in France begins rearmament (autumn); Rome-Berlin Axis
1937	Chamberlain accelerates rearmament
1938	*Anschluss* (March); Munich Conference (September)
1939	British change of policy leads to greater liaison with France (February)

1 Introduction

> **KEY ISSUE** What was Appeasement?

Appeasement is most commonly associated with the policy of Neville Chamberlain, British Prime Minister from 1937 to 1940. More specifically, it is associated with the Munich crisis of 1938 and the failure to prevent the outbreak of war in 1939. Indeed so far from preventing war, appeasement appeared to actually to bring it about by encouraging Hitler to make greater demands. Quite clearly the policy failed and it failed spectacularly. Because of this it came to be seen as a dishonourable policy, a policy of peace at any price, a policy of craven acquiescence in the demands of a bullying dictator - it became, in fact, a byword for cowardice, a pejorative term. But this is not what the word meant in origin - most dictionaries usually define appeasement as pacification or conciliation - and that is what Foreign Secretary Anthony Eden meant in 1936 when he stated to the House of Commons, 'it is the appeasement of Europe as a whole that we have constantly before us' - meaning, quite simply, that he wished to make Europe a peaceful place. British policy was in fact mainly just that - keeping the peace - and it was prepared to do that by satisfying reasonable grievances, by making concessions to avoid war.

Indeed before 1938 appeasement was a policy approved by practically everyone. It had been the principal characteristic of British foreign policy from Versailles onwards, for it did not take long for anti-German feeling in Britain to subside after the war and, when it did, a feeling grew that the harshness of the Treaty could be progressively modified by negotiation and concession. Opposition to the French occupation of the Ruhr (1923), support for the Dawes and Young Plans (1924 and 1929) and the Locarno Treaty (1925), the removal of weapons inspectors from Germany(1927), the withdrawal of troops from the Rhineland (1930) and the virtual cancellation of reparations in 1932 were all part of a piece: remove Germany's grievances and there will be no war. In addition, by the 1930s most historians were contending that Germany was not solely responsible for the war, thus removing any remaining moral justification for the Treaty.

Appeasement, then, was not a policy of peace at any price; it was in fact a rational policy based on a wide variety of considerations, considerations that will be discussed later in the chapter. Appeasement was, above all, a British policy, but in the later 1930s it was a policy that the French also came to adopt. Quite why is the subject of the next section.

2 French Foreign Policy Explained

> **KEY ISSUE** Why was French foreign policy so indecisive in the inter-war period?

a) The 1920s

France had been devastated by the effects of the First World War. Apart from the colossal debts incurred (4 billion dollars to the USA and 3 billion to Britain), about ten per cent of her territory had been laid waste, affecting some of the most valuable industrial and agricultural resources. In addition and more importantly, a million and half men had been killed (ten per cent of active males - the highest proportion of all the major belligerents) and another 3 million wounded. This not only had an adverse demographic effect on a static and ageing population but it also left deep psychological scars: parents, grandparents, wives, girlfriends, brothers, sisters, and children all experienced the grief of lost loved ones - there can have been few who were untouched by the experience.

Accordingly there was immense pressure on the Prime Minister, Georges Clemenceau, whose nickname was 'the Tiger', to deliver a punitive peace which would render Germany harmless in the future. But so far from being the tough negotiator of textbook fame, Clemenceau abandoned all thought of dismembering Germany or of a permanent French occupation of the Rhineland on the flimsy assurance of an Anglo-American guarantee (which never came to pass). Thus he succumbed to a lenient peace and was roundly criticised, especially by Marshal Ferdinand Foch, for giving away too much. Frenchmen could be forgiven for seeing Clemenceau as more of a pussy cat than a tiger.

The peace was accepted by both parliament and people with grim resignation and by the end of 1919 many saw the peace merely as an armistice, a truce for 20 years as the famous cartoon opposite so poignantly implied. For in truth the German problem had not been resolved: Germany's larger population (60 million as opposed to 40 million - but a ratio of two to one in the age group 20-34 by 1940) and greater industrial capacity meant that in any rerun of the contest the Germans would probably come out on top.

France therefore needed allies and, in the absence of a strong League of Nations and a deal with Britain, signed a series of bilateral agreements through the 1920s with Belgium (1920), Poland (1921 and 1925), Czechoslovakia (1924), Rumania (1926) and Yugoslavia (1927) - the last three being known as the 'Little Entente', though how valuable these were is a moot point.

In addition it was decided to take a tough line against Germany and rigidly enforce the terms of Versailles. The famous occupation of the Ruhr in 1923 was just the last, most spectacular example of this policy - it is often forgotten that French troops were sent across the Rhine to enforce German compliance several times during the course of 1920-21.

However, the Ruhr occupation turned out to be a defeat for France herself as well as a disaster for Germany (see page 11). It paved the way for a period of appeasement signalled by the Dawes Plan of 1924 and the Locarno Agreements of 1925 and later the Young Plan of 1929 and the evacuation of French troops from the Rhineland in 1930. The policy of conciliation and compromise is most associated with Aristide Briand, who was foreign minister between 1925 and 1931. However, as time passed obstacles to his policy came to the fore.

The death of Stresemann and the Wall Street Crash (both 1929) created instability and unease. Yet whereas in the aftermath of Versailles French strategy had been based on offensive action to counter the German threat, by 1929 policy had changed completely. It was now entirely defensive. This was signalled by the start of the Maginot Line in that year, though the much derided fortifications were not designed to protect the whole of France, just Alsace Lorraine; the German attack was always expected to come through Belgium, where the bulk of the French army was to be. However, the problem lay not so much with the Maginot Line itself, but with the passive and defensive mentality it came to represent. The French wrongly believed in the superiority of defence over attack - which had

A cartoon from *The Daily Herald*, 1919

of course been true for the previous war but which took insufficient account of technological developments since, especially the offensive potential of tanks and aircraft.

b) The 1930s

The new decade was ushered in with disappointment at the failure of the League of Nations to cope with Japan's invasion of Manchuria in 1931. From the French point of view it made little sense to agree to arms reductions at the long-awaited Disarmament Conference in this climate, especially when the German government continued to flout the Versailles agreement, and especially when Germany came under 'new and dangerous management'[1] from 1933.

France had been less affected by the Depression in the years 1929-1932 (she was less dependent on trade) but it struck later, peaking in 1935, and there was no recovery until 1938. Historians have identified a precipitate collapse in French standing between 1933 and 1937 coinciding with this economic crisis. There was (always) considerable ministerial instability (11 governments between 1932 and 1935 - all of them weak coalitions) and France was politically divided (some would say it had been since 1789!). This was because of the rival ideologies of Communism and Fascism which in 1935 made France look first one way (to Fascist Italy in the Stresa Front in March and for a military agreement in June) then the other (to the Soviet Union for an alliance also in June). There was rarely any continuity or consistency in foreign affairs and as a result particular policies were often not carried through to their logical conclusion: paralysis could be the result. This, together with a general feeling of revulsion against war, weakened French reactions to Hitler and in fact encouraged him by presenting no opposition.

The remilitarisation of the Rhineland in 1936 (see page 38) came as no surprise in France and caused little consternation. However, it did cause the Belgians to revoke their military accord and opt for neutrality, thus presenting the French high command with a dilemma over their strategy (they took the easy way out and decided to change nothing). Other setbacks followed: as a consequence of the Abyssinian crisis (see page 33) Italy drifted towards Germany, a process accelerated by the Spanish Civil War; negotiations with the Soviet Union seemed to be going nowhere; and Britain remained as non-commital as ever. The threat to French security was by now very real - the German army was thought to be certainly the equal of the French and the air force superior. Accordingly, in the autumn of 1936 the left-wing Popular Front government launched the first serious substantial rearmament effort in the interwar period: 31 billion francs were spent over the next three years. 1938 brought more tension as the Austrians were annexed and the Czechs dismembered. By this time, French policy was in the hands of foreign minster

Georges Bonnet and Prime Minister Édouard Daladier. However, whereas Bonnet was an arch-appeaser, Daladier was not - he was disgusted by the Munich settlement and for him it was something of a turning point. However, French policy remained one of appeasement until Britain finally made a firm continental commitment to France in February 1939. At this point Daladier stepped up rearmament and was quick to agree to military discussions with the British Chiefs of Staff. Now French opinion hardened against Hitler, and after February 1939 French policy was characterised by a resolution and confidence that had not been present for many years.

c) Analysis

Most analysis of French foreign policy in the interwar period has been coloured by France's rapid collapse in 1940. This was such a disaster that (so the argument goes) it had to be the outcome of deep-seated political, social and economic weaknesses. Accordingly historians have searched for all manner of divisions and examples of decadence, corruption, pacifism and incompetence - and they have not been disappointed. From this point of view, France deserved defeat in 1940 - she had it coming to her. However, if perhaps the defeat was largely just the result of superior German military strategy in the month of May 1940, then this whole approach is quite false and the debate it has generated is meaningless. Now this is not to say that France did not have weaknesses - they were there in abundance - but it is just to say that their importance has been exaggerated by the all-too-familiar mistake of reading history backwards.

Nevertheless there is no doubt that the politics of government in the Third Republic were quite chaotic. 43 prime ministers between 1917 and 1940 does not create much political continuity in terms of policy and decision-making. Why was this? The answer seems to be the voting system of proportional representation which generated a large number of parties, none of which could obtain a majority. For instance, in 1938 there were fully 17 political groups in the Chamber from which some sort of government had to be formed. This sort of situation meant that governments had to be cobbled together by compromise and concession; clearly most were fragile coalitions with a short life. There was also, as we have already indicated, a considerable political divide between the right and the left which severely damaged foreign policy. On the left there was a strong strain of pacifism, and a revulsion against war among the population at large (particularly the peasantry). This in turn served to hamper any attempt at rearmament.

It took a change of heart by the left in 1936 to actually get rearmament under way. It was the Popular Front government which recognised the threat Hitler posed and dropped the policy of pacifism. Of course it turned out to be a case of too little, too late, but it is rather

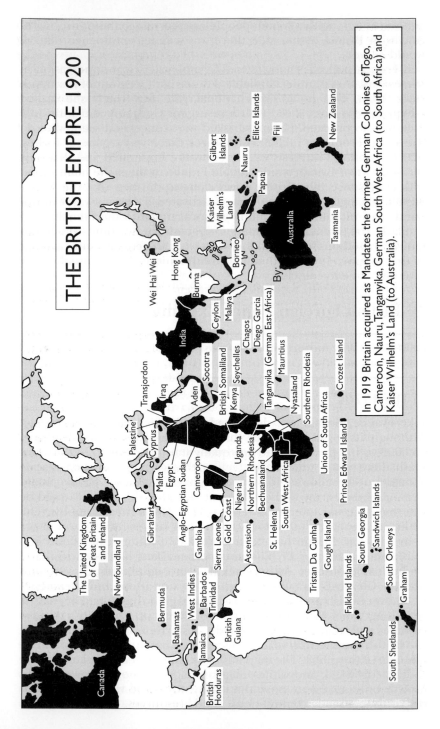

THE BRITISH EMPIRE 1920

In 1919 Britain acquired as Mandates the former German Colonies of Togo, Cameroon, Nauru, Tanganyika, German South West Africa (to South Africa) and Kaiser Wilhelm's Land (to Australia).

responsibilities were in fact a logistical nightmare. A General Staff minute of 1921 stated; 'our liabilities are so vast ... that to assess them must be largely a matter of conjecture'.[2] For instance, apart from the defence of the British Isles, the (self-governing) dominions of Australia and New Zealand expected to be defended by the Royal Navy, Palestine alone tied down 20,000 troops during a rebellion in 1938, and the bulk of forces had to be stationed in India where the growing tide of nationalism seemed to threaten the very basis of British rule. Britain could not possibly defend such a disparate, widespread set of territories. Moreover, the Empire was not a coherent structure; there was no common economic policy, no agreed system of decision-making, no co-ordinated defence structure. The larger the Empire became, the more impressive it looked on paper, but the more difficult it became to administer and defend.

It was fortunate for Britain that in the immediate aftermath of the war this was not a major problem. With some justification the cabinet agreed in August 1919 that

It should be assumed ... that the British Empire will not be engaged in any great war during the next ten years, and that no Expeditionary Force is required for this purpose.[3]

Dramatic cuts were made in armed forces expenditure, e.g. from £692 million in 1919-1920 to £115 million by 1922, and this Ten Year Rule, as it was known, came to be extended beyond 1929. Rearmament did not in fact get under way again until 1934.

From the moment the Peace of Paris was signed, the British government was revisionist. As early as March 1919 Lloyd George warned against treating Germany too harshly and the influential economist J.M. Keynes emphasised that European economic prosperity as a whole very much depended upon German economic recovery. The British approach to the peace, then, was rather different from that of the French as it was based on economic self-interest rather than security. In this context it is not surprising that there was a clash over the Ruhr occupation in 1923 (see page 19). Indeed Britain increasingly saw itself as neutral between France and Germany rather than allied to the former against the latter. After Locarno it was hoped that Europe could safely be left to solve her own problems, but by the early 1930s it was clear that detachment might not keep the peace. As the world situation deteriorated, rocked by the repercussions of the Wall Street Crash, Britain could not stand idly by. The British government still believed it had a special moral role as a leader in world affairs, a legacy of that Victorian self-confidence which would be slow to fade.

b) The 1930s

As we have already indicated, when the Ten Year Rule was up in 1929, it was agreed to extend it. In any event the onset of the Depression made rearmament a financial impossibility. The crucial event that changed British policy was Japan's invasion of Manchuria in 1931. Japan had been an ally of Britain's since 1902 but, under pressure from the USA, Lloyd George had given up the Japanese alliance in 1921 at the Washington Conference. This had deprived Britain of any means of influencing Japanese policy without substituting any compensating support from the USA. The cabinet reluctantly concluded that the Ten Year Rule should be cancelled on 23 March 1932 and in 1933 a Defence Requirements Committee (D.R.C.) was established to advise on strategy and rearmament. Manchuria was clearly a defeat for the League of Nations and privately politicians were aware of its ineffectuality. However, the League was very popular with the public and in this new era of full democracy (all men and women over 21 had the vote from 1928) the government had to take much more notice of public opinion.

Rearmament on the other hand did not appear to be popular; in the East Fulham by-election of 1933 the Conservative candidate who advocated rearmament turned a majority of 14,000 into a defeat by 5,000 at the hands of his Labour opponent who supported disarmament (though of course other issues were involved). In 1935 the League of Nations Union's 'Peace Ballot' which advocated international disarmament was endorsed by more than 11 million people. Stanley Baldwin, the Conservative leader, became convinced that rapid rearmament would mean defeat at the polls in the next general election (which took place at the end of 1935). 'I give you my word there will be no great armaments,' Baldwin told the electorate in 1935, even though he did plan some rearmament.

The D.R.C. produced its first report in February 1934 and identified Germany as 'the ultimate potential enemy', pushing Japan and naval considerations into second place. It recommended the establishment of an expeditionary force but the cabinet felt that public opinion would be hostile to this. Instead priority was given to building up the R.A.F., which the cabinet's dominant figure, the Chancellor Neville Chamberlain, saw as the best deterrent against Germany. The government and the public had exaggerated fears of the destructive potential of air power in any future conflict, encapsulated in Baldwin's remark in 1932 that 'the bomber will always get through'. Later the Ministry of Health would estimate 600,000 British deaths in the first six months of war, when in fact the total in the whole six years of the Second World War was 60,000. The Defence White Paper of March 1935 declared that the principal role of the R.A.F. was 'to provide for protection of the United Kingdom and particularly London against air attack'[4] and priority was given to the production of bombers whose role would be to attack German cities in retaliation for any air assault on Britain. (Of course all of this overlooked the fact that the Luftwaffe did not have the range to reach Britain, just as the R.A.F. could not reach Berlin!)

The D.R.C. reported again in November 1935 by which time Hitler's rearmament programme was public knowledge and the Abyssinian crisis was turning Mussolini, a potential ally, into a potential enemy. It stated:

1 It is a cardinal requirement of our National and Imperial security that our foreign policy should be so conducted as to avoid the possible development of a situation in which we might be confronted simultaneously with the hostility of Japan in the Far East, Germany in the West,
5 and any power on the main line of communication between the two.[5]

In March 1936 its conclusions formed the basis of a four-year plan for rearmament which Chamberlain accelerated when he came into office. Expenditure leapt from £185 million in 1936 to £719 million in 1939 (see the table on page 43).

However, aware of current British weakness and acting on the advice of the Committee and Defence Chiefs, Stanley Baldwin, Prime Minister from June 1935, did his best to avoid any crisis. In this context he and his predecessor MacDonald acquiesced in Hitler's reintroduction of conscription and remilitarisation of the Rhineland, attached little importance to the Stresa declaration, signed a naval agreement with Germany, which upset the French, did little to prevent Mussolini taking Abyssinia (but enough to lose his friendship), and stayed out of the Spanish Civil War, thus giving the dictators a free hand. With hindsight, these policy decisions (if they can be so called) look like failures but they have to be seen in the context of Britain's military weakness and global concerns. Where perhaps Baldwin did err was in being too ready to accommodate public opinion - he tended to follow rather than mould it, but perhaps that is one of the functions of a democratic politician. Another problem was the fact that the government seemed to be caught off guard by each successive crisis and was constantly reacting to events rather than having any influence over how they might develop. When he became Prime Minister in May 1937 Neville Chamberlain was determined to inject more vigour and purpose in foreign affairs: he was prepared to take the initiative. Policy changed from passive to active appeasement.

Thus Chamberlain assumed much more responsibility for foreign affairs than had his predecessor, hoping to produce what he called a 'Grand Settlement' of international problems, to create 'a lasting European peace' through a concert orchestrated by Britain and involving France, Germany and Italy. This was based on the (false) assumption that Hitler was a reasonable man and that he could get a deal with Germany involving the possible return of colonies, an air pact and some resolution of Germany's grievances in eastern Europe. Chamberlain did not want to make any firm guarantees to France, he did not trust the USSR but he did put some (misplaced) trust in Mussolini, whom he felt might restrain Hitler. Early in 1938 the foreign secretary, Eden, resigned not because he opposed appease-

- Profile -

(ARTHUR) NEVILLE CHAMBERLAIN (1869-1940)

Neville Chamberlain was born in Birmingham in 1869, the son of the famous radical politician Joseph Chamberlain. After considerable experience in local government in Birmingham, he became Director General of National Service in 1917 and an MP in 1918. For much of the 1920s he was Minister of Health and for much of the 1930s he was Chancellor of the Exchequer. He became Prime Minister in 1937. He was noted for his clear thinking, mastery of detail and hard work, but also for his impatience with criticism, his certainty in his own beliefs and his disdain for those who disagreed with him. As Prime Minister he devoted much of his energy to foreign policy, though he had little experience of it. He is of course primarily associated with the policy of Appeasement which found its basis in his personal fear of war, his appreciation of Britain's limitations and his belief that Germany's grievances were genuine. As he said at the time of Munich:

> Armed conflict is a nightmare to me ... I shall not give up hope of a peaceful solution, or abandon my efforts for peace, as long as any chance for peace remains
>
> from his radio broadcast 27th September 1938

But he misread Hitler and his policy failed. With the invasion of Poland a year later, Chamberlain was forced to declare war. He acknowledged the failure of his policy:

> 1 This is a sad day for all of us, and to none is it sadder than to me. Everything that I have worked for, everything that I have hoped for, everything that I believed in during my public life, has crashed into ruins ... I trust I may live to see the day when Hitlerism has been
> 5 destroyed, and a liberated Europe has been re-established.
>
> from his address to Parliament September 3rd 1939

Sadly he did not live to see the end of Hitler. He stood down as Prime Minister in May 1940 to make way for Winston Churchill, and he died of cancer, a broken man, on November 9th 1940.

ment (though he opposed negotiations with Mussolini) but because of Chamberlain's determination to conduct foreign policy himself.

Chamberlain's determination to achieve a peaceful settlement was to some extent influenced by wild overestimates of German rearmament and strength from the Chiefs of Staff. A particularly gloomy review of the international situation was produced by them in June 1937 in which the Italian threat in the Mediterranean was added to that of Germany in Europe and Japan in the Far East: 'the outstanding feature of the present situation is the increasing probability that a war started in one of these three areas may extend to one or both of the other two'.[6] Their conclusion was that until rearmament was further advanced, it should be the first task of foreign policy to diminish the number of Britain's enemies. The policy of 'appeasement' can only be fully understood if the military context is also fully understood. Since the summer of 1937, the Treasury too had been demanding a more positive attitude to Germany by the Foreign Office. In December 1937 Sir Thomas Inskip, a goverment minister with responsibility for coordinating defence, presented his *Interim Report on Defence Expenditure in Future Years*, inspired by Treasury fears that expenditure was exceeding limitations. It is evident from the report that the stability of the British economy was considered of vital importance if Britain were to fight because it was believed the next encounter would again be a long war of attrition. Based on this premise, the priorities for defence were to be (in order of importance):

i) military preparation sufficient to repulse air attacks
ii) the preservation of trade routes for the supply of food and raw materials
iii) the defence of the Empire
iv) the defence of any power or powers with whom Britain might be allied.

As in 1934, priority was given to the R.A.F. but cabinet now changed the strategy. Priority was given to the construction of a fighter force; the bombers were now of less importance. This was justified on the grounds that the development of radar made the interception of enemy bombers feasible. In January 1938 the Chiefs of Staff presented a review which reiterated what had been stated in the summer memorandum:

1 Naval, Military and Air Forces in their present stage of development, are still far from sufficient to meet our defensive commitments, which now extend from western Europe, through the Mediterranean to the Far East ... We cannot foresee the time when our defence forces will be
5 strong enough to safeguard our territory, trade and vital interests against Germany, Italy and Japan simultaneously.[7]

These observations together with the financial constraints placed on rearmament no doubt convinced the Prime Minister that the conciliation of Germany and Italy was to be preferred to confrontation. Indeed they presented him with little choice.

Chamberlain had come into office determined to take the initiative but the *Anschluss* with Austria in March 1938 took him by surprise (as it did Hitler!). He did not object to the union but he disliked the way it had happened. Still he felt it made appeasement all the more urgent. In a statement to the House of Commons on March 24th,

Chamberlain stated that the next crisis would be over Czechoslovakia and while he could not guarantee that state (nor automatically come to the aid of France, her ally) he did point out that, if a war did break out, Britain might not be able to stay out. Of course, this veiled threat was meant to be a deterrent; Chamberlain's real aim was to achieve a peaceful settlement, and his three flights to Germany in the autumn indicate the lengths he was prepared to go to. However, the real problem was that Chamberlain took Hitler's demand for the Sudetenland at face value; he believed Hitler just wanted to unite all Germans. After meeting him for the first time, he wrote to his sister: 'I got the impression that here was a man who could be relied on when he had given his word'.[8] But just a week later Hitler had raised the stakes. War now seemed likely and Chamberlain even undertook to support France in war if the French decided to fight for the Czechs. However, his real reluctance can be gauged from his broadcast to the nation on the evening of 27 September 1938:

1 How horrible, fantastic, incredible it is that we should be digging
   trenches and trying on gas masks here because of a quarrel in a far-away
   country between people of whom we know nothing ... war is a fearful
   thing, and we must be very clear, before we embark on it, that it is really
5 the great issues that are at stake.[9]

It is clear from this broadcast that Chamberlain did not want a war over this issue (see the critical cartoon opposite) and when the opportunity came for a conference at Munich, he leapt at it. When he returned with 'peace for our time', he was greeted as a hero by both press and people, and was bombarded with letters of congratulation (over 40,000) and gifts (including very many umbrellas - see the flattering cartoon from *Punch* opposite). However, in the House of Commons the debate over the settlement elicited strong criticisms from Churchill, Attlee and others. Although the government won the vote, the debate was seen as a defeat. The policy looked as threadbare as it actually was. Indeed the criticism articulated in the Commons presaged a dramatic change of mood in Britain, which had already been anticipated by divisions in cabinet.

For Britain, and to a lesser extent France, Munich turned out to be the limit of the policy of concession. Peace at any price was never the policy of Chamberlain or his cabinet; the British government would not accept German domination of Europe. Chamberlain still placed some faith in negotiation and believed he might be able to influence Hitler through Mussolini but his visit to Rome in January 1939 achieved little.

Indeed it was the Foreign Secretary, Halifax, who took the lead in urging a tougher policy towards Germany; on 25 January he warned that Hitler might attack in the West. On 1 February the cabinet agreed that Britain must go to war if Germany invaded either Holland or Switzerland and agreed to staff talks with the French. On

A cartoon from Punch, *September 1938*

A cartoon by Gabriel, September 1938

6 February Chamberlain declared that 'any threat to the vital interests of France from whatever quarter it came must evoke the immediate cooperation of Great Britain'.[10] Even more important, a paper by the Chiefs of Staff on February 20 argued that home defence might have to include a share in the defence of French territory. On February 22 the Cabinet agreed to prepare an army of eight divisions for despatch to the continent. Thus British policy was in the process of undergoing a dramatic change in February 1939. The previous assumption had been that Hitler's aims were limited. It was now feared that Hitler's ultimate aim was the domination of Europe, and he might have to be stopped. Chamberlain still believed that Hitler could be stopped without war. Now the democracies were better prepared, the Prime Minister felt, Hitler would be deterred. How wrong he was!

c) Analysis

There was actually something of a contradiction at the heart of British foreign policy. Britain wanted to be left alone, undisturbed by continental Europe, to make secure the immense British Empire and develop British trade and prosperity. Britain wished to avoid alliances at all costs - they were a diplomatic liability - and adopted an increasingly isolationist outlook. However, at the same time, Britain was not prepared to abandon its influence and prestige and it felt it had a moral duty to intervene in world affairs, to put them right when it considered that it was necessary to do so. Britain adopted what was essentially an *ad hoc* policy, that is to say Britain adopted a flexible and pragmatic approach to problems as they arose - some problems were confronted; others ignored. This gave the impression that British policy was incoherent, indecisive and unpredictable. Now of course this generalisation does not necessarily apply across 20 years of policy-making to each of the prime ministers and foreign secretaries involved, but there is some basis to it. As we have seen British policy was largely governed by three major concerns and, at the risk of some repetition, it is worth looking at them again:

i) the revision of the Versailles Treaty to mollify Germany
ii) public opinion
iii) extensive global commitments and military and economic weakness.

Many soon felt that the Versailles treaty was too harsh and was storing up trouble for the future. We have already referred to Lloyd George's reservations about the treaty (see page 71). Most Liberals were opposed to the Treaty and the Fabian Beatrice Webb denounced it as 'a harsh and brutal peace'. There was a groundswell for revision - and not just on the left. This of course was the basis for the deterioration of Anglo-French relations. Britain and France saw the treaty in completely different ways; for example, whereas Britain saw the

League of Nations as a symbol and a forum for modifying the Treaty, France saw it as the guardian of peace and security. Failure to reconcile Germany was commonly attributed to French rather that to German ill will. Although reparations were swept away before the Nazis came to power, the feeling was that too little had been done. Moreover by the 1930s the notion of War Guilt that had been applied to Germany gave way to the view that no one country had been responsible for the war, a view summed up in Lloyd George's observation: 'the nations, slithered over the brink into the seething cauldron of war'. This explains why Hitler's more aggressive approach was greeted by an acceleration of concessions, rather than resistance. Hitler's coming to power, it appeared, resulted from insufficient appeasement. Many in Britain felt Hitler had a good case, and many were also won over by his anti-communist stance and saw him as a useful barrier to Soviet expansion.

In the 1930s both MacDonald (Prime Minister 1929-35) and Baldwin (1935-7) were primarily concerned with a narrow view of British problems, neatly summed up by the latter's biographer, G.M.Young, who commented that 'where France was thinking of her dead, Baldwin was thinking of our unemployed'.[11] Baldwin was particularly concerned to respond to public opinion or, rather, had a shrewd eye for popularity and votes; for instance in 1935 he created a Minister for League of Nations Affairs, despite private cabinet misgivings about the effectiveness of the League.

Indeed public opinion was an important factor in the formation of British foreign policy. The memories of the horrors of trench warfare led to a 'never again' mentality summed up in the famous Oxford Union (university debating society) vote in February 1933 'that this House would not fight for King and Country'. Public opposition to rearmament held the process back. In any event many felt it would only antagonise Hitler unnecessarily. In addition, the need to respond to public opinion by supporting the League of Nations against Mussolini over Abyssinia had a disastrous effect on that policy as it neither stopped Mussolini nor retained his good will (see page 36). Fear of the bomber was another pressure on government policy. The destruction of Guernica by German bombs in the Spanish Civil War made a deep impression on people and Chamberlain saw for himself the vulnerability of London when he flew for the first time in 1938. But of course the truth was, the whole of the British Empire was vulnerable - as Chamberlain himself said: 'we are a very rich and very vulnerable Empire'.[12]

Britain's international commitments were summarised in a Foreign Office memorandum of 1926. Apart from obligations as a member of the League, and as a signatory to the Paris, Washington and Locarno treaties, there were commitments to Egypt, Abyssinia, to the Middle East, to Portugal, to the entire Commonwealth and Empire, which consisted of Australia and New Zealand as well as India and

Singapore, large areas of Africa and the Caribbean and numerous places in between. It was in fact an impossible task and the Chiefs of Staff finally stated as much in 1938. Whereas Germany, Japan and Italy could focus their revision in distinct regions, Britain had to adopt a world-wide strategy. The real problem of course was that Britain simply did not possess the military or economic strength to defend such a far-flung Empire and could not assert herself when challenged. The army was spread thin, everywhere weak, nowhere strong. The navy was still substantial but had to take second place in the 1930s to the development of the R.A.F., which had to face the immediate threat of Nazi Germany. In these circumstanes, Japanese expansion in the Far East simply had to be allowed to take its course.

All of this begs the question - what alternatives, what choices, did Britain have in foreign affairs when confronted with aggressive, expansionist dictatorships in the 1930s? The answer would seem to be, precious few. Both the Treasury and the Chiefs of Staff supported appeasement and were happy with the Munich settlement. General Ironside stated: 'Chamberlain is of course right. We have not got the means of defending ourselves and he knows it ... We cannot expose ourselves now to a German attack. We simply commit suicide if we do'.[13]

Britain was not divided politically like France. The National Government had a large majority and the Labour Party, largely paci-fist until 1936 but in favour of rearmament after that, did not create obstructive opposition. Accordingly appeasement was not controver-sial until 1938. Up to that time Hitler asked for nothing that the British were not, in the end, willing to grant. Even Churchill welcomed government inaction over the remilitarisation of the Rhineland in 1936 (and of course had approved cuts in the armed forces as Chancellor in the 1920s). But appeasement was not peace at any price - it was a policy of adjustment and accommodation, but accommodation that did not disturb British interests. The govern-ment was not prepared to give Germany a free hand in eastern Europe, or the right to tear up the Versailles settlement on its own terms. Thus Chamberlain was 'hoping for the best [by appeasing Hitler] while preparing for the worst [by rearming].'[14] However, there was an almost infinite capacity for self-deception in Britain concerning the nature of the Nazi regime and the personality of its leader (though not in the case of Labour leaders Dalton and Bevin, and later Attlee). Chamberlain did not understand Hitler; he did not understand that his concessions generated contempt rather than grat-itude. 'Our opponents are little worms. I saw them at Munich' was Hitler's summation. Limited, negotiated adjustments to the Versailles Treaty was not what Hitler wanted, but Chamberlain could not see that. Indeed throughout 1939 he continued to appease; the guar-antee to Poland was more Halifax's doing; Chamberlain kept Churchill out of the government for fear of antagonising Hitler; he did not make a serious attempt to negotiate with Stalin for the same reason (as well as because of fundamental ideological reservations); he was prepared to negotiate over Poland despite the guarantee; and he was slow to react when Hitler invaded that country on 1 September 1939.

So, were there any alternatives to appeasement? Chamberlain could have had an alliance with France and possibly one with the Soviet Union. However, Churchill's alternative belligerent approach, some might say, was based on a romantic, unrealistic view of Britain's position in the world, and all-out rearmament would have had serious economic repercussions. Moreover, would Hitler have been deflected from his purpose? By waiting for a year after Munich Britain was better prepared - the country was united, better armed and had the support of the Empire and the moral support of neutrals (though it had lost the support of the Czech army). Chamberlain was a decent man who had lost relatives in the slaughter of 1914-18 (including his best friend, his cousin, Norman) and did not want young men of the next generation to suffer the same fate. But he was up against a man who was quite prepared to risk another war and who placed his long-term goals ahead of all other considerations. Once again we return to the central point: Hitler caused the war. However, how far he was encouraged by Chamberlain's policy of appeasement and whether or not he could have been stopped earlier remains a lively topic of debate. To the historiography of appeasement we now turn.

4 Appeasement: The Debate

> **KEY ISSUES** Has the historical debate shed more heat than light on the matter? Do we now have a better understanding of Appeasement?

After Britain's defeat in France and retreat from Dunkirk in 1940, Michael Foot and two other journalists published a short book called *Guilty Men* which blamed the defeat on the politicians of the 1930s. It was their failure to stand up to Hitler that had brought matters to where they were in 1940. When in 1945 the full horror of the Nazi regime was revealed, this only served to further discredit those politicians who had tried to negotiate and compromise with the German dictator. In 1948 Winston Chuchill published the first volume of his Second World War memoirs, *The Gathering Storm,* in which he endorsed the judgements made by the authors of *Guilty Men*: 'there was never a war more easy to stop;'[15] it was an 'unnecessary war' brought about by the failure to stop Hitler rearming. Thus there grew up the idea that there had been a series of 'lost opportunities' to stop Hitler, in 1936 over the Rhineland, in 1938 over Czechoslovakia and even in the summer of 1939 by the reformation of the *Entente* with

Russia and France. Churchill contended that Baldwin had failed to rearm because he feared electoral defeat and Chamberlain had been fooled by Hitler, who had pretended to want a settlement. Sir Lewis Namier was more blunt (1950): 'the appeasers aided Hitler's work'.[16] It was Churchill's work that firmly discredited the policy of appeasement and created a historical consensus that lasted for a quarter of a century, reaching its apogee in Martin Gilbert and Richard Gott's indictment of Chamberlain, *The Appeasers*, in 1963. In this work the policy was characterised as dishonourable submission, the pursuit of peace at any price.

Yet within a few years revisionism had begun with D.C. Watts' article in the *Political Quarterly*.[17] Even before that A.J.P. Taylor had shaken everything up with his 1961 book *The Origins of the Second World War*; though controversial because of what he had to say about Hitler, what he had to say about Munich was equally provocative. He described the settlement as 'a triumph for all that was best and most enlightened in British life; a triumph for those who had preached equal justice between peoples; a triumph for those who had courageously denounced the harshness and short-sightedness of Versailles'.[18] In 1966 Martin Gilbert drew back from his previous position in a new book entitled *The Roots of Appeasement*, which identified appeasement as the objective of British policy since 1919; however, he still condemned Chamberlain for continuing with the policy after 1937. Two years later Keith Robbins published a self-styled 'transitional book', *Munich 1938*, which saw the settlement as 'the desire to avoid another war' rather than peace at any price.

What accelerated the pace of revisionism was the introduction of the 30 Year Rule in 1968, which made available the cabinet minutes and government papers of the 1930s. Now historians had a better picture of the context in which the politicians of the 1930s were operating and were able to appreciate both the complexities and constraints. In 1972 Correlli Barnett in *The Collapse of British Power* and Michael Howard in *The Continental Commitment* both highlighted the problems Britain faced in defending her vast Empire in the 1930s. Barnett went further and stated that the Empire could only realistically be defended in war by turning to the USA for help, which is of course what happened.

The rehabilitation of Chamberlain began in 1975 with the publication of Maurice Cowling's *The Impact of Hitler: British Politics and British Policy, 1933-1940*, which stressed the responsible nature of Chamberlain's policy; it was above all realistic about Britain's interests, commitments and resources. He went on to criticise Churchill for continuing the war against British interests after 1940, a position which had also been adopted by Barnett. These works presaged the Chamberlain versus Churchill debate of the '80s and '90s. In 1979, G.C. Peden published *British Rearmament and the Treasury 1932-1939*, which argued that the concerns about the cost of rearmament and a long war were well founded and in 1981 Paul Kennedy's *The Realities Behind Diplomacy* summarised historians' work on the domestic pressures which helped to shape appeasement policies. By the 1980s we were much more aware of the difficult strategic, economic and domestic context in which the politicians of the 1930s had been working.

The rehabilitation of Chamberlain continued in the early 1980s through the writings of David Dilks, though his major biography, *Neville Chamberlain, 1869-1929* (1984) has yet to reach the 1930s as the title suggests. In 1989, John Charmley published what is perhaps the most complete defence of Chamberlain, *Chamberlain and the Lost Peace.* He followed this up with an attack on Churchill in *Churchill: The End of Glory* (1993) and completed the trilogy with *Churchill's Grand Alliance* (1995). Charmley's position is that appeasement was justified because war with Germany would be ruinous if we won or lost (as it turned out to be), and had Hitler been a normal statesman who would have been prepared to compromise and show patience, all would have been well. Thus criticism should be confined to Hitler rather than Chamberlain. Moreover, Churchill's decision to fight on in 1940 handed world ascendancy to the United States, eastern Europe to the Soviet Union and spelt the end of the British Empire.

However, Churchill has had his defenders and Chamberlain still has his critics. Richard Cockett in *Twilight of the Truth* (1989) demonstrated how Chamberlain manipulated the press to suppress opposition to his policy and Andrew Roberts in his 1991 biography of Lord Halifax demonstrated that it was the Foreign Secretary who was responsible for abandoning appeasement after Munich, as Chamberlain became an increasingly isolated figure. Indeed R.A.C. Parker in *Chamberlain and Appeasement* (1993) made it clear that Chamberlain stuck to appeasement long after it was evident to almost everyone else that Hitler could not be trusted. However, Parker's central point, that there were alternatives to appeasement such as a military alliance with France and Russia, is only viable if we assume Hitler could be stopped by it. If we accept that he was determined to gain *lebensraum* in the East regardless of any opposition, then war was bound to come sooner or later. All roads seem to lead back to Hitler.

As you can see, appeasement is clearly a highly complex issue and the historical debate is ongoing. While we now better understand why the policy was adopted, we cannot avoid the fact that it was a failure - and it failed because Hitler had a programme of his own and he was not prepared to change course. It did, however, buy the democracies valuable time and there is no doubt that Chamberlain's motives were honourable - he wanted to save a generation of young men from slaughter - but his judgement of Hitler's personality and how events were unfolding was mistaken. Churchill told him after the Munich crisis that he had been given a choice between 'dishonour and war: you chose dishonour, but you will still have war'[19] and he was proved right. Similarly, and earlier, in February 1938, Ernest Bevin, the trade union leader, stated:

1 I have never believed from the first day when Hitler came to office but that he intended at the right moment and when he was strong enough, to wage war in the world. Neither do I believe, with that kind of philosophy that there is any possibility to arrive at agreements with Hitler and
5 Mussolini.[20]

Chamberlain may have been a poor judge of Hitler, but not everyone was; and as 1939 progressed more and more people came to see what he was really like.

References
1 P. Bell, *The Origins of the Second World War in Europe* (Longman, 1997), p. 104.
2 Quoted in P. Hayes, *The Twentieth Century* (A & C. Black, 1978), p. 212.
3 Quoted in A. Boxer, *Appeasement* (Collins, 1998), p. 15.
4 Ibid, p. 16.
5 Quoted in R. Overy, *The Origins of the Second World War* (Longman, 1998), p. 18.
6 Quoted in A.Crozier, *The Causes of the Second World War* (Blackwell, 1997), p. 14.
7 Ibid, p. 135.
8 Quoted in Boxer, *Appeasement*, p. 36.
9 Transcript in *The Times*, September 28, 1938.
10 Quoted in Bell, *Origins*, p. 278.
11 Quoted in Hayes, *The Twentieth Century*, p. 237.
12 Quoted in Overy, *Origins*, p. 16.
13 Quoted in R. Pearce, 'Appeasement' in the *History Review*, March, 1998, p. 28.
14 Ibid, p. 29.
15 Quoted in Bell, *Origins*, p. 47.
16 Ibid.
17 See Crozier, *Causes*, p. 233.
18 Ibid, p. 227.
19 Quotation in Pearce, *History Review*, p. 29.
20 Quotation in Bell, *Origins*, p. 117.

Source-based questions on 'Appeasement'

1   Versailles and Appeasement
Study the cartoons on pages 65 and 77. Answer the following questions:

a) Sum up the essential message of the British cartoon of 1919 on page 65. Why did it prove to be so prophetic? (10 marks)

b) The cartoons on page 77 reflect markedly differing views of Chamberlain. Explain them. (10 marks)

Structured Question on 'Appeasement'

a) What was Appeasement? (4 marks)
b) Explain why Britain and France pursued such a policy. (6 marks)
c) Assess the importance of the historical debate in furthering our understanding of this issue. (10 marks)

Summary Diagram
Appeasement

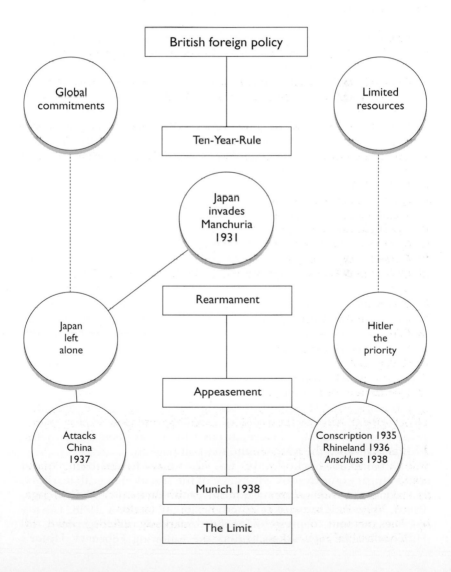

6 The Outbreak of War

POINTS TO CONSIDER

This chapter deals with the transformation of the European diplomatic situation between October 1938 and March 1939, Soviet foreign policy, the Nazi-Soviet Pact, the invasion of Poland, and the outbreak of war. You should consider why the Soviets signed a deal with Hitler, and why Britain and France went to war over Poland.

KEY DATES

1938 Munich Conference (September)
1939 Change of policy in Britain (February); Hitler marches into Prague (March); Britain and France issue a guarantee to Poland (March); Hitler plans an attack on Poland (April); Mussolini marches into Albania (April); Britain and France issue guarantees to Greece and Rumania (April); Pact of Steel (May); Nazi-Soviet Pact (August); Hitler invades Poland (September); Britain and France declare war on Germany (September)

1 From Munich to Memel, October 1938-March 1939

> **KEY ISSUE** In what ways was the European diplomatic situation transformed in this brief period?

One of the most ominous by-products of the Munich settlement was that it reinforced Hitler's reputation for infallibility, to himself as well as to those around him. As we have already indicated, the Führer felt cheated by the settlement over Czechoslovakia - in the bunker in 1945 he regretted not starting the war a year earlier over this issue - and he was probably jealous of the praise heaped on Chamberlain for saving the world from war. On 10 October he privately declared his intention of annexing what remained of Czechoslovakia and on October 21st approved a plan for its 'liquidation' (see page 57) as well as for 'taking possession of Memel,'[1] a German city which had been taken by the Lithuanians after the war (see the map on page 8).

The rump of Czechoslovakia was now unstable and both Poland and Hungary quickly took advantage of the situation to grab territory. Slovakia was given greater autonomy and when the Slovak deputy Prime Minister, Durcansky, visited Berlin in October 1938, Göring encouraged him to press for Slovak independence, as indeed did Hitler when he met Slovak leaders the following February. Hitler's plan was to make Czechoslovakia break up from within.

In the aftermath of the Munich settlement, Chamberlain still hoped for a general settlement and, on November 6th, a Franco-German declaration was signed along similar lines to the separate British document that Chamberlain had so proudly displayed on his return from Munich. However, the Nazi attack on the Jews on the night of 9 November - known as Crystal Night because of all the broken glass from ransacked shops - brought condemnation in the British press and led to another decisive shift in British public opinion, a shift that led eventually to the dramatic change in British policy which has already been referred to (see page 76). In January 1939 the British government received a series of disturbing reports about German ambitions against Czechoslovakia, Memel and Poland which were finally taken seriously. The previous assumption, that Hitler's aims were limited, was now discarded. In addition the joint planning sub-committee produced a much more favourable assessment of Britain's strategic position by emphasising that the German economy was too weak to sustain a long war and, under pressure from Halifax, the government finally took steps to resist Germany and support France. French policy, which had been in limbo since Munich, could now finally take shape.

In the meantime, Hitler had been making attempts to turn Poland into a German satellite. He did not initially aim at partition or conquest because his main aim remained a showdown with Bolshevik Russia and the conquest of *lebensraum*. Hitler felt that because the Poles were anti-communist and anti-Russian, joint action would be possible. For many years he had suggested an anti-Soviet alliance but the Poles thought better of it. After Munich, the Nazi regime stepped up the pace. On 24 October 1938 Ribbentrop put Germany's proposals for the recovery of Danzig (a German city under League of Nations control) and a road and rail link through the 'corridor' (see the map on page 8) to Joseph Lipski, the Polish ambassador, but met with little response. These proposals were repeated when Poland's foreign minister Beck visited Berlin on 5-6 January 1939, but again they met with an evasive response, despite Hitler's hint of Polish acquisitions in the Ukraine in the future. Ribbentrop then went to Warsaw on 26 January to press for a decision, but again without success. The Poles did not wish to become German puppets - nor did they wish to upset the Russians by joining the Anti-Comintern Pact. However, it would appear that these demands were a test of Polish willingness to act as a German satellite, and the Polish government's failure to commit to Hitler forced the German leader to dramatically alter his policy and consider Polish annihilation. But prior to that decision, the Führer was faced with the break up of Czechoslovakia.

Although Hitler had been working for the destruction of Czechoslovakia, once again the timing of the occurence was not of his own making and it took him by surprise. On 6 March, in an effort to recreate a measure of unity, President Hacha of Czechoslovakia dismissed the government of Ruthenia and on the 9th he did the same to Slovakia. Hitler acted quickly to arrange a declaration of Slovak independence and on March 15 agreed to receive President Hacha only to tell him that the German army was taking over his country. After suffering a stroke - probably as a result of Hitler's tirade - Hacha signed a piece of paper handing Bohemia and Moravia over to Hitler and on 16 March the two provinces were declared a protectorate of Germany. German troops and tanks were already there.

These events created a profound sense of shock in Britain since there could be no pretence any more about uniting Germans - the Czechs were definitely not German. It now seemed that Hitler's aims were unlimited. Initially, Chamberlain's reaction was lame but on the 17th in a speech in Birmingham he was more combative, complaining of Hitler's broken promises, posing a series of rhetorical questions about the fate of other small states and ending by stating Britain would not flinch from resisting a challenge. Clearly the influence of Halifax was at work here, but Chamberlain felt the deception very personally. On 18 March he told the Cabinet, 'no reliance could be placed on any of the assurances given by the Nazi leaders.'[2] The message was clear: Hitler could not be trusted and German attempts to dominate Europe had to be resisted - but the next time since nothing could now be done about Czechoslovakia.

But Hitler was not listening. On 19 March he requested that the Lithuanian government hand over Memel and four days later it did so. This also created alarm in Britain, where there was a fear that the Poles might succumb to German influence, so on 27 March Halifax proposed that a guarantee be offered to Poland. The issue though was not Poland. As Chamberlain himself put it, 'our object is to check and defeat Germany's attempt at world domination.'[3] On 30 March the guarantee (to which France adhered) was offered and accepted at once by the Poles and on 31 March British policy, which had really changed over a month before, was finally made public. The Prime Minister announced in the House of Commons:

1   in the event of any action which clearly threatened Polish independence,
    and which the Polish Government accordingly considered it vital to
    resist with their national forces, His Majesty's Government would feel
    themselves bound at once to lend the Polish Government all support in
5   their power.[4]

Although the wording left open the possibility of border changes, the guarantee was meant to act solely as a deterrent and little was done in the aftermath to give the agreement any substance. This probably sent the wrong signal to Hitler. After all there was little Britain and France could do to give Poland direct assistance. In any event, the pledge to Poland had quite the opposite effect on him. Instead of making him cautious and take a step back, it simply infuriated him and caused him to comment, 'I'll cook them a stew that they'll choke on.'[5] In retrospect it is clear that Hitler's occupation of Prague and Memel was mistaken, but his impatience and the logic of his plans seem to have robbed him of caution; from now on he seemed unable to break his own momentum. Chamberlain, for his part, still hoped to keep the peace, but we should not underestimate the emotions of a disappointed man; even Churchill conceded that Chamberlain was a man who did not like to be cheated. If Chamberlain had misjudged Hitler, then it is also true to say that Hitler misjudged Chamberlain.

2 The Nazi-Soviet Pact

> **KEY ISSUE** What were the aims of Soviet foreign policy in this period? How did Hitler and Stalin, arch-enemies for so long, come to sign an agreement?

a) The Aftermath of the Guarantee

The six months between the Munich settlement and the Anglo-French guarantee to Poland had witnessed dramatic changes. A new European situation took shape. Britain and France had come together and were determined to stop Hitler dominating Europe. Hitler for his part was more determined then ever to press on with his plans for expansion. It seems that the only effect the deterrent had was the opposite to that intended; Hitler always reacted to any move to curb his plans with anger and even greater wilfullness.

On April 1st 1939, the day after Chamberlain had publicly announced the guarantee to Poland, Hitler demonstrated his anger with Britain in a speech at Wilhelmshaven for the launching of the battleship Tirpitz, by threatening to scrap the Anglo-German Naval Agreement. Two days later (April 3rd) he ordered Keitel to draw up military preparations for an attack on Poland at any time from 1st September 1939. On 6 April negotiations with Poland were suddenly broken off. Operation White, as it was called, was ready by April 11th, though it is clear that the plan was to entail a limited war confined to the objective of Poland: Germany was not yet ready for a wider war.

The tension continued to rise: on 7 April Mussolini marched his army into Albania, choosing the right moment for maximum effect. *Il Duce* had been a little miffed that Hitler had not informed him in advance of his occupation of Prague; there was an element of petulance in his response and an attempt to get even. However, to the western democracies the action seemed to imply that the dictatorships were in some way coordinating their activities and immediately (on April 13th) Britain and France issued guarantees to both Greece and Rumania. The following day the U.S. President, Franklin D.

Roosevelt, addressed a rather naive letter to the dictators calling upon them to agree not to attack 31 countries which he listed by name. This elicited from Hitler what was by all accounts one of his finest (and longest) speeches in which his protestations of innocence were proclaimed and his real intentions not at all. Addressing the Reichstag on 28 April he responded by citing all the countries the President had mentioned and, to the mirth of those present, he went through them one by one with a straight face, pointing out that he did not have any designs on Ireland or Syria or Persia or Turkey or Spain or Palestine etc; however, the real sting in the speech had come at the beginning with the denunciation of the 1934 Non-Aggression Pact with Poland (he did not name Poland in the list) and the 1935 Anglo-German Naval Agreement.

The following month Hitler and Mussolini signed a full-blown military alliance - the so-called Pact of Steel (22 May). Japan could not be persuaded to join what would be a Triple Alliance and Italy only reluctantly signed, fearing its somewhat open-ended commitment. Hitler hoped this would keep Britain and France neutral, and it is true that *Il Duce* had been making noisy demands for the French territories of Tunis and Savoy. However, privately both Mussolini and his son-in-law the Foreign minister, Count Ciano, made it very clear that Italy would not be ready for war for three or four years (though this was not stated in the alliance). Still, that did fit in with Hitler's long-term plans, as he expressed to his commanders the following day:

1 It is not Danzig that is at stake. For us it is a matter of expanding our living space in the East and making food supplies secure and also solving the problem of the Baltic States ... If fate forces us into a showdown with the West it is good to possess a largish area in the East ...we are
5 left with the decision: *to attack Poland at the first suitable opportunity* ... There will be war ... [but] it must not come to a simultaneous showdown with the West [France and England]. If it is not definitely certain that a German-Polish conflict will not lead to war with the West [we] must strive for a short war. But the government must, however, also
10 prepare for a war of from ten to fifteen years' duration ... The Führer lays down that ... the armaments programme will be completed by 1943 or 1944.[6]

It is clear that Hitler had decided on war with Poland even if it came to a showdown with England and France, though that is not what he wanted. And the destruction of Poland was his objective not the recovery of lost territory. Throughout June and July detailed plans and military arrangements were put in train, while the German press resumed its anti-Polish campaign. However, the diplomatic focus now turned to the Soviet Union, as Stalin suddenly found himself courted by both sides.

b) Soviet Foreign Policy

Since the Bolshevik Revolution of 1917 and the establishment of the alternative communist system, with all its international implications, the Soviet Union had been something of a pariah in western eyes. It was not suprising that both the isolated Russians and the defeated Germans should make common cause in the 1920s; however, with Hitler coming to power, everything had changed (see page 23). Stalin, who emerged as leader from the power struggle after Lenin's death in 1924, was above all a pragmatist, and ideological considerations diminished in Soviet foreign policy in the 1930s - though there remained something of a dualism at the heart of Soviet policy: while the Foreign Ministry attempted to normalise relations with capitalist governments, the Comintern encouraged their revolutionary overthrow! Still, Stalin wished to avoid war at all costs but the search for security was hampered by his personal caution and the USSR's suspicion of all capitalist powers. Whether this represents a policy of keeping all options open or a policy of indecision depends upon your perspective.

Thus there were contradictions in Soviet policy, further exacerbated by the rise of the alternative ideology of fascism. The Soviets found themselves caught between the alternatives of Nazi Germany and the western democracies. So, on the one hand, there was the ideological policy of anti-fascism, on the other, the expediency of peaceful coexistence with the Nazis; on the one hand, the hope of common cause with Britain and France, on the other the reality of those countries' appeasement of the Nazi regime.

Hitler's repudiation of Rapallo led the Soviet Central Committee to pass a resolution in favour of collective security in December 1933, though the door was always left open to reconciliation with Germany as Stalin's speech in January 1934 made clear. However, the Soviets took ideology seriously (the regime was after all built on ideology itself) and nowhere was the content of *Mein Kampf* studied more closely. In December 1933 Litvinov, the foreign secretary, stated in a speech to the Supreme Soviet in reference to Hitler and the Nazis:

1   The founder of this party devoted a book to developing in detail his conception of German foreign policy. According to this Germany was not only to reconquer all the territories of which it had been deprived by the Versailles treaty, not only to conquer lands where there was a
5   German minority, but by fire and sword to cut a road for expansion to the East, which was not to stop at the Soviet frontier, and to enslave the Soviet people ...[7]

Similarily Premier Molotov also referred publicly to *Mein Kampf's* policy of territorial conquest in his speeches to the Congress of Soviets in January 1935 and to the Supreme Soviet in January 1936. Accordingly, in pursuit of collective security, the USSR joined the League of Nations in September 1934, and signed mutual assistance

JOSEPH STALIN (1879-1953)

Stalin, who was born Joseph Dzhugashvili in Georgia in 1879, trained to be a priest but became a Bolshevik instead. After the 1917 Revolution he rose to become the general secretary to the Central Committee (1922), from which position he was able to outmanouevre his opponents after Lenin's death (1924) and become sole leader. He coined the phrase 'socialism in one country' and attempted to make Russia self-sufficient by a series of Five Year Plans. He stated:

> We are fifty or a hundred years behind the advanced countries. We must make good this distance in ten years. Either we do it or they will crush us.
>
> from a speech in 1931

Stalin trusted no one and his paranoia led to mass executions and purges of both the party and the armed forces. His foreign policy was cautious and he surprised everyone by making a deal with Hitler in 1939, though he had little choice. He was true to the Pact and said at the time:

> The Soviet Government takes the pact very seriously. I can guarantee on my word of honour that the Soviet Union would not betray its partner.
>
> Stalin to Ribbentrop August 23rd 1939

When Hitler turned on Stalin in 1941, the latter was momentarily stunned. He recovered, refused to contemplate peace and eventually fought back, defeating the Germans, enlarging the Soviet Union and spreading communism throughout Eastern Europe. From 1945 he consolidated his hold on his satellite states behind an 'iron curtain', thus helping to begin the Cold War. His paranoia contributed to its intensification.

Stalin was clearly one of Russia's most successful rulers but the kindly epithet 'Uncle Joe' belied his savage nature. When he became ill in 1953 his immediate entourage would not call a doctor as they feared another purge if he recovered. He died on March 5th of that year.

pacts with both France and Czechoslovakia in May 1935. Later that year the Seventh Congress of the Comintern proclaimed the new doctrine of the Popular Front against fascism. However, behind the public face of Soviet policy there was an alternative strategy characterised by confidential discussions with Germany about the possibility of improving relations. The Germans themselves made numerous offers of a substantial expansion of trade which the Russians took seriously, while at the same time Moscow's policy of collective security foundered over the democracies' lack of enthusiasm. Basically the Soviets were fearful of German intentions but at the same time deeply suspicious of Britain and France. Accordingly Soviet policy seemed to be presented with two rather unattractive alternatives - to coexist with the unfriendly West or seek *détente* with the hostile Nazis. Clearly the one undermined the other and the Soviets fell between two stools by pursuing both at the same time. While Litvinov was implacably opposed to the Nazi regime, Stalin, Molotov and the Politburo were more flexible and in April 1935 a trade credit agreement was signed with Germany and another in May 1936. Molotov's speech of January 1936, though it made reference to *Mein Kempf*, did not rule out the possibility of co-existence. However, 1936 saw Hitler occupy the Rhineland, give aid to Franco in the Spanish Civil War, launch a major anti-communist propaganda campaign at Nuremberg in September and sign the Anti-Comintern Pact with Japan in November. The omens for co-existence did not look good, but then nor did the alternative.

As we have suggested, in no other country was the threat of Hitler's ambitions taken more seriously but the problem for Moscow was that the policy of collective security seemed to be going nowhere. The French resisted Soviet efforts to transform the Franco-Soviet Pact into a real military alliance; the League's failure over Abysinnia confirmed its impotence; and Anglo-French appeasement of Hitler made Moscow fear that the western powers would be happy if Hitler turned against the Soviet Union. Hence Soviet policy was in a sort of limbo. In view of all this uncertainty, it made sense to keep all options open and in this context, in January 1937, the Politburo actually approved formal negotiations with Nazi Germany - but these came to nothing.

1938 was dominated by the Czech crisis (see page 52). The *Anschluss* in March came as no surprise in Moscow and it was anticipated that Czechoslovakia would be next. From the beginning to the end of this crisis the Soviets campaigned for international resistance to Hitler's designs on Czechoslovakia, urged the Czechs to stand firm and made it clear it would honour the pact if France did. However, as early as May 1938 when Litvinov met his French and British counterparts, Bonnet and Halifax, in Geneva, he came away with the distinct impression that Anglo-French support for the Czechs was very doubtful. In his speech in June he once again referred to Hitler's expansionist aims and continued to put pressure on London and

Paris. However, Polish and Romanian opposition to the passage of Soviet troops across their territory made the possibliltiy of an agreement unlikely. Litvinov became certain that the Czechs would be betrayed, though briefly at the end of September, between Chamberlain's second and third visits to Hitler, war did seem a possiblitiy (see page 54). The Russians mobilised, but soon after the Munich Conference took place and the Soviets (as well as the Czechs) were excluded. The snub felt by the Soviets at this exclusion and their mistrust of the democracies are well illustrated by the cartoon in which Daladier and Chamberlain are depicted as policemen directing Hitler towards the U.S.S.R.

Despite this setback the USSR did not abandon its collective security policy and, after Hitler occupied Prague in March 1939, it seemed a real possibility. In April 1939 the Soviets proposed a Soviet-British-French triple alliance, but now the Soviet aim was not deterrence but a firm military alliance to gain support in the event of war.

b) The Pact

From mid 1937 until the spring of 1939 little happened in Soviet-German relations. However, in 1939 Hitler's policy changed and Nazi Germany began its quest for a pact with the USSR in order to prevent a Soviet alliance with the democracies and to obtain Soviet neutrality in the event of a Polish-German war. The initiative did not come from Moscow. Since the collapse of the Soviet Union in 1991 more sources have become available and recent research has shown that Stalin's

Soviet cartoon

speech of March 1939 did not constitute a signal for reconciliation with Berlin. Similarly Litvinov's dismissal as foreign minister in May, hitherto seen as a significant gesture to the Nazis because he was Jewish, is also no longer seen in the same light. Soviet policy afterwards did not change at all. The USSR continued to pursue the democracies for an alliance. A more credible explanation of his dismissal is Stalin's wish to assert greater control over foreign policy at a time when he believed the world was on the brink of war. Litvinov had frequently been at odds with the leadership; he was replaced by the more amenable Molotov.

Although German accounts depict the Soviets as being desperate for a deal with Berlin, Russian accounts paint a very different picture. Germany's advances were rebuffed in May 1939 when Molotov spoke of the welcomed prospect of a deal with the western democracies. He rebuffed them again at the end of June. After a lull the Germans made advances again at the end of July. This time Molotov was prepared to listen. Why? It appears he was becoming increasingly disillusioned by negotiations with Britain and France. In fact he stated on July 17, 'it seems nothing will come of these endless negotiations'[8] - and endless they were, a point so well brought out by A.J.P Taylor in his book over 35 years ago:

1   The diplomatic exchanges show that the delays came from the West and that the Soviet Government answered with almost breathtaking speed. The British made their first tentative suggestions on 15 April; the Soviet counter proposal [for a triple alliance] came two days later, on 17 April.
5   The British took three weeks before designing an answer on 9 May; the Soviet delay was then five days. The British took thirteen days; the Soviet government answered within twenty-four hours. The British next needed nine days; the Soviets two. Five more days for the British; one day for the Russians. Eight days on the British side; Soviet answer on the same day. British delay of six days; Soviet answer the same day ... If dates mean anything, the British were spinning things out, the Russians were anxious to conclude.[9]

Moscow did not really know what to make of German advances; Soviet policy was indecisive and passive. Despite German pressure Molotov remained non-committal. In any event the Anglo-French delegation finally arrived on 10 August to discuss a potential alliance. Criticisms of this mission are well known: the delegates went by ship rather than plane, the negotiators were of low rank and status, the British had no written powers to negotiate, the French did but had no powers to sign anything, and neither Britain nor France had any strategic and operational plans for a joint war against Germany. However, negotiations really broke down over the lack of Polish consent to the passage of Soviet forces across their territory.

Not until these negotiations collapsed did Molotov seriously entertain the German approaches. Already on 8 August the Germans had proposed an updating of Rapallo and made references to 'German Poland' and 'Russian Poland' - words clearly designed to suggest that some form of territorial compensation at Poland's expense was on offer. By now Hitler had a timetable and was determined to attack Poland before the autumn rains. On 12 August Keitel was told to be prepared to attack on 26 August. The Germans were in a hurry.

With the collapse of the Anglo-French negotiations the clear goal of Soviet foreign policy now became the avoidance of a war with Nazi Germany at all costs, but it appears that this was very much a last-minute decision. On 17 August, probably at Stalin's request, Molotov agreed that Ribbentrop, the German foreign minister, could come to Moscow on 26-27 August, but this did not fit in with Hitler's timetable. So on 21 August the German ambassasdor, Schulenburg, presented Molotov with an urgent personal message from Hitler to Stalin for an earlier visit. Two hours later Stalin replied personally that Ribbentrop could come on 23 August.

After Ribbentrop's arrival it only took two meetings to reach agreement. The Nazi-Soviet Pact of 23 August 1939 stunned the world; it was a most remarkable reversal of previously held ideological animosity. The agreement consisted of a non-aggression pact and a secret additional protocol, which stated:

1. In the event of a territorial and political rearrangement in the areas belonging to the Baltic states (Finland, Estonia, Latvia, Lithuania), the northern boundary of Lithuania shall represent the boundary of the spheres of influence of Germany and the USSR ...
2. In the event of a territorial rearrangement of the area belonging to the Polish state the spheres of influence of Germany and the USSR shall be bounded approximately by the line of the rivers Narew, Vistula and San.[10]

Cartoon by David Low, September 1939

This pact has usually been misrepresented for, as A.J.P. Taylor pointed out many years ago, 'the Pact was neither an alliance nor an agreement for the partition of Poland'[11] - i.e. the partition was not a guaranteed outcome: nothing was certain on August 23rd 1939 except that Russia would be neutral in the event of a German attack on Poland. When that would be, and what the outcome would be, was not altogether clear at the time. There was no discussion of any coordinated military action. In fact Ribbentrop actually had to tell the Russians to occupy their 'sphere of interest' once war was under way! The Poles collapsed so quickly that the Russians were taken by surprise and were not in a position to move in until 17 September, over two weeks after hostilities began.

c) Conclusion

What then are we to make of Soviet foreign policy in the run-up to the Second World War? Its main characteristics appear to be caution, indecision and the ability to face in two different directions at once!

The problem for Russia was that it was isolated, disliked by both the capitalist democracies and the Fascist dictatorships. Hitler represented a greater threat to the Soviets so it made sense to pursue a policy of collective security, but because this was never really achieved the door had to be left open to the Germans. There is no doubt that behind the attitudes of Britain and France there lay a long-standing distrust of the Soviet Union and Bolshevism. Chamberlain in particular was vehemently anti-communist. Thus Russia remained isolated and could not afford to provoke the Germans. This perhaps explains Stalin's somewhat less than wholehearted support for the left in the Spanish Civil War: he might not have wanted to antagonise Hitler. Moreover, it should be remembered that Russia was undergoing rapid and necessary industrialisation. At the same time, in the period 1937-8, the Red Army was more than decimated by a series of military purges which swept away almost all its senior staff and commanding officers. The reasons why Stalin should do this at such a tense time are difficult to unravel. Perhaps the purges were designed to create greater unity, but they seem to reflect Stalin's personal paranoia and also developed a momentum of their own. Weakening the army gave added impetus to the desire to avoid war.

Ideally Stalin would have liked a deal with the democracies - or so he is reported to have said on 7 September 1939:

We would have preferred an agreement with the so-called democratic countries, hence we entered negotiations with them, but Britain and France wanted us to be their hired hand ... and without pay.'[12]

In truth Britain and France could not enter into an alliance with the Soviet Union without alienating most of the states of Eastern Europe. And the Poles, to whom Britain and France were committed, would not have an alliance with Stalin at any price. Thus Britain and France offered the Soviet Union nothing except perhaps war, and possibly war on her own. Stalin wished to avoid a European war at all costs - he already had to face Japanese aggression in the East. He therefore had little choice. The pact was the Soviet Union's only policy option - it was all that was on offer and it offered the prospect of no war (and territorial expansion, though this was not fully appreciated at the time). It is surprising that so much criticism has been levelled at Stalin for taking what was not just the best deal, it was the only deal. Once again, however, it was Hitler who was taking the initiative: it was Hitler's timetable, it was Hitler's deal. The Nazi-Soviet Pact was a decisive event on the road to war. The Anglo-French deterrent against Germany, feeble from the start, was now completely undermined. There could be no possibility of military action in support of Poland from the east. The way was open for a German attack on Poland.

3 The Attack on Poland

> **KEY ISSUE** Why did Hitler's invasion of Poland lead to a general war?

With the Pact, Hitler now felt he was free to attack Poland: he did not believe Britain and France could do anything about it and he did not believe they would declare war. Indeed he stated to his generals on August 22nd:

> England and France have undertaken obligations which neither is in a position to fulfil. There is no real rearmament in England, but only propaganda.[13]

However, Chamberlain wrote to Hitler on the same day and stated quite categorically:

> Apparently the announcement of a German-Soviet Agreement is taken in some quarters in Berlin to indicate that intervention by Great Britain on behalf of Poland is no longer a contingency that need be reckoned with. No greater mistake could be made.[14]

When the official announcement of the Pact was made Hitler awaited the democracies' response but there was none. In fact he misunderstood British policy completely - Britain's real concern was not Poland, but Hitler himself. Still he took comfort from those parts of Chamberlain's letter that reflected an obvious unwillingness to go to war, and on 25 August he offered negotiations, and stressed his willingness to solve the tiresome problem of the Polish corridor, a problem which, in his words, 'must be solved' - which in reality left little scope for any meaningful discussion. After all, from Hitler's point of view, unlike the Sudetenland this territory had been German until it had been taken away by the flawed Treaty of Versailles: Germany's claim was a good one. Thus Hitler was momentarily taken aback later that day when he heard that Britain and Poland had finally signed a full military alliance. He also learnt of Italian reservations. Ciano believed Britain would go to war and Mussolini began to get cold feet. These two factors made Hitler postpone the attack on Poland until September 1st (a delay that gave him 25 extra divisions) and he went through the charade of negotiating with the Poles, though his self-styled 'generous offer' of discussions was never seriously intended and took the form of an ultimatum. Halifax and Chamberlain were still receptive to a diplomatic solution and Mussolini also tried his hand on August 31st, but Hitler would not be deterred. In fact he had been delighted when the Poles declined to negotiate - he felt this gave him a propaganda victory - and at 12.30 p.m. on August 31st he signed the Directive No. 1 for the conduct of War. In the early morning of September 1st 1939 the German attack on Poland began. Hitler was determined to go to war (and of course the Poles were determined to resist).

There was a long delay between the German attack on Poland on 1 September and the British declaration of war on 3 September, and Chamberlain suffered some criticism in the House of Commons for being slow to send an ultimatum. However, it does appear that this was caused by trying to finalise evacuation and mobilsation plans and by trying to coordinate a response with the French. France too declared war on 3 September, albeit 6 hours later. Hitler was momentarily stunned by this (as late as 31 August Goebbels recorded in his diary that 'the Führer did not believe England will intervene') - it was neither the war he expected nor the one he wanted - and he seemed to be unhappy with Ribbentrop, who had constantly assured him that the democracies were bluffing. Still, he only had himself to blame; always the gambler, he had always been prepared to take the risk of a general war. On August 29 Göring had pleaded with him not to play *va banque* (an expression referring to gambling against the banker - i.e. against the odds), but Hitler had replied: 'throughout my life I have always played *va banque*.' [15]

So the Second World War broke out in September 1939 and, although it was the product of a long period of international crises, its immediate roots were Hitler's miscalculation that he could get his own way in eastern Europe without a general war. He failed to realise that Britain and France viewed the Polish crisis in terms of their global concerns and great power status and he greatly underestimated allied military strength. Allied intelligence, on the other hand, was more realistic - the military balance was considered not unfavourable and because the continued pace of allied rearmament would become economically impossible it was felt that this was the best time to challenge Germany. By 1942, it was argued, Germany might be too powerful, which of course was Hitler's plan.

Chamberlain hoped for a negotiated settlement to the last, and both the British and the French put pressure on the Poles in the last weeks of August to make some concessions. But the Poles would not be moved. So what we have at the beginning of September 1939 is the conjunction of these three elements that account for the outbreak of war:

1. Hitler's mistaken belief that the democracies were weak and irresolute
2. Britain and France's fears for their great power status, and
3. Poland's determination to stand firm.

Of course Hitler did not miscalculate in the sense that he did have a short victorious war with Poland and the democracies did absolutely nothing to stop him. He also chose the moment to attack them, and with some success as we shall see in the next chapter.

Accounts of the origins of the Second World War in Europe some-times end in September 1939 but this is a mistake. For many histo-rians the war did not become a world war until 1941 with the entry of Japan and the U.S.A. But there is another reason for arguing that the real Second World War did not begin until 1941. If we consider that the war was caused by Hitler's ambitions, then his main ambition was to invade Russia, and only by following events down to that point in June 1941 can this argument be fully appreciated (the purpose of the next chapter). If we focus too much on September 1939, then the role of the Poles and that of Britain and France loom too large and give an artificial picture. Only briefly did others seize the initiative - for the most part it was held by Hitler. September 1939, then, was only a stage - albeit an important one - on the road to a truly world war.

4 Conclusion

> **KEY ISSUE** Why did Britain and France go to war over Poland and why was Hitler so determined to invade?

Could war have been avoided in 1939? The answer is yes, but it pre-supposes several unlikely events. One is that Hitler would have pulled back from the brink and would have been satisfied with his gains of 1938 - an unlikely scenario. Another is that the Poles would have simply rolled over and allowed the German leader to dismember their country as the Czechs had been forced to do - another unlikely scenario. Or thirdly that Britain and France would have appeased again, looked the other way and allowed Hitler a free hand.

Quite why Britain and France risked everything to stop Hitler in Eastern Europe is a topic of lively debate. After all, if the western democracies went to war in 1939 to preserve their great power status which they believed to be at risk, they surely lost it by doing so. Preserving the balance of power in Europe had always been an aim of British foreign policy - from the time of Louis XIV, through Napoleon to the First World War. German domination of the continent would, it was felt, threaten Britain's great power status and, in the long term, represent a threat to the British Empire (especially since Germany was allied to the colonial predators, Italy and Japan). In addition, there is no doubt that there was a rising tide of national sentiment against Hitler in both Britain and France that made it easier for their governments to confront him; and it was the case that these countries had by 1939 the full support of their empires and the sympathy of the United States. Moreover, it was also considered a propitious moment both in terms of the improved readiness of their armed forces, and in terms of the military balance which it was believed could only deteriorate as time went on. British rearmament was geared to peak in 1939-40 - by mid 1939 Britain could feel some measure of security (the radar system was in operation, for instance) but because this balance could not be expected to last, the democracies were trapped in a timetable of their own making. The British military attaché in Berlin supplied reliable evidence that Germany would not be able to risk, let alone sustain, a major conflict for any length of time in 1939/40. Reports suggested Germany would not be ready for any major conflict for a number of years - and we know this to be true. All Hitler's planning was geared to 1942/3.

The years 1939-40, then, were the only time the allies thought they could confront Hitler with any reasonable chance of success - so they did. However, that does not make them responsible for the war. They wanted Hitler to back down, but he would not. The question then remains why Hitler was so determined to press on. After all, this was the wrong time for him to undertake a major war.

There are a number of reasons why Hitler displayed mounting impatience and wilfullness from 1938 onwards. One factor was the economic problems raised by rearmament and Hitler's fear that others' rearmament would whittle away at his lead and make his position impossible by 1942/3. Hitler did not know that the democracies' rearmament programmes could not continue at the same rate, just as the democracies did not know that German rearmament was faltering. Rearmament went forward in Germany in a rather haphazard way. After the 'May Crisis' of 1938 (see page 53) Hitler began construction of defensive fortifications in the west to meet the French threat. After Munich, he ordered a fivefold (!) increase in the air force to meet any British threat and in January 1939 he approved the construction of 10 battleships (the 'Z Plan') to be ready by 1943/4 for a world war. The problem with all this was that Germany had neither the resources nor the manpower to keep up with this programme (in February 1939 it was estimated that there was already a shortage of a million workers). As Hitler himself said in August 1939 'our economic situation is such that we can only hold out for a few more years ... we must act.'[16] Moreover, Hitler was not at all systematic: he continually shifted priorities. He tended to encourage each of the service chiefs to press ahead with achieving his own goals, with little co-ordination and with little reference to what was actually possible. Because he felt he was under time pressure he began to tele-scope his programme - for instance, the expansion of the navy was given the go-ahead prior to the army securing the continental empire. The combination of a head start over the other powers with the lack of the means to expand production over the long term led to the idea that it was better to risk war now. It also led inevitably to the strategy of *blitzkrieg* - a short but decisive campaign of rapid movement - and to the idea of plundering the defeated countries to augment German resources (for instance, three armoured divisions in the French campaign were equipped with Czech vehicles). Of course, this argu-ment - that Hitler was pushed into war by economic pressures - is that of the *structuralists* which we referred to in Chapter 1 (see page 3). Although it is an approach that has not been widely embraced by historians, it clearly has a basis in fact and cannot be dismissed entirely.

Germany then was only ready for the war of September 1st 1939 not that of September 3rd. Only half the army's 102 divisions were battle-ready and the navy was distinctly inferior to that of Britain and even to that of France. Although the air force was strong, the Polish campaign used up fully one half of Germany's total ammunition stock and left her vulnerable (an attack from the West might well have been successful in the autumn of 1939). Hence *blitzkrieg* was the only option, but it was bound to fail if the war became protracted.

There are other reasons for Hitler's growing impatience in 1939. One was his increased sense of self-confidence, which had been fed by success after success - he felt he could turn his obsessions into reality by sheer willpower; another was his desire to capitalise on public goodwill (there was no general desire for war in Germany in 1939 but the *Anschluss* and the occupation of Czechoslovakia had gone a long way towards restoring German pride); and yet another was his growing concern about his health which has already been referred to (see page 59) and even concerns about assassination. Indeed he himself stated on 22 August 1939:

1 Essentially all depends upon me, upon my existence, because of my political talents. Furthermore, the fact [is] that no one will ever again have the confidence of the whole German people as I have. There will probably never again in the future be a man with more authority than I
5 have. My existence is therefore a factor of great value. But I can be elim-inated at any time by a criminal or a lunatic.[17]

The strength of Hitler's position in 1939 enabled him to seriously consider implementing his ideological aims. Once again his roots in the nineteenth century racial philosophies of Social Darwinism and nationalism came to the fore as they had done when he wrote *Mein Kampf*. Hitler came to relish the prospect of a war - for him it was 'the

ultimate goal of politics', its 'strongest and most classic manifesta-
tion.'[18] Indeed, he believed peace was harmful and that struggle was
everything. The World War, Hitler repeated, had never ended for
him: on 23 November 1939 referring to the First World War, he
stated, 'today the second act of this drama is being written.'[19] The
connection between Hitler and both the 1914-18 war and the pre-war
world is clear: eastern expansion had been the aim of the Pan
German League as early as 1894, as it was for Moltke 20 years later in
1914. However, we should not overplay the continuity between the
First and Second World Wars in this sense, since Hitler had far more
sweeping victories in mind and a new racial order brought about not
by any natural process but by the murderous brutality of his homicidal
anti-Semitism.

References

1 Quoted in Joachim C. Fest, *Hitler* (Pelican, 1973), p. 844.
2 Quoted in P. Bell, *The Origins of the Second World War in Europe* (Longman,
   1997), p. 286.
3 Ibid. p. 287.
4 Ibid.
5 Quoted in Fest, *Hitler*, p. 860.
6 Quoted in Noakes and Pridham, *Nazism*, pp. 737-8.
7 Quoted in G. Roberts, *The Soviet Union and the Origins of the Second World
   War* (Macmillan, 1996), p. 15.
8 Ibid, p. 82.
9 A.J.P. Taylor, *The Origins of the Second World War* (Penguin, 1964), p. 282.
10 Quoted in Roberts, *The Soviet Union*, p. 92 - some adjustments were made
   to the territorial provisions in the agreement of 28 September (see page
   106).
11 Taylor, *Origins*, p. 318.
12 Quoted in Roberts, *Soviet Union*, p. 95.
13 Quoted in Noakes and Pridham, *Nazism*, p. 741.
14 Ibid.
15 Ibid. p. 754.
16 Quoted in Noakes and Pridham, *Nazism*, p. 740.
17 Ibid.
18 Quoted in Fest, *Hitler*, p. 901.
19 Ibid. p. 915.

Answering essay questions on 'The Outbreak of War'

Consider the following examples:
1. 'Hitler's foreign policy in the years 1936-1939 rested upon no long-
   term strategy, but upon the shrewd manipulation of opportunities as
   they arose.' To what extent do you agree with this view?
2. Why, having seen peace apparently secured in September 1938, did the
   nations of Europe find themselves at war in Septermber 1939?

3. 'The betrayal of Czechoslovakia by Britain and France in September 1938 made a general European war more likely, but it was the Nazi-Soviet defence Pact of August 1939 which made it inevitable.' Discuss.

For a discussion of a suggested approach to essay writing, see page 45. Essay 1 is very much the subject matter of the previous chapters as it requires you to discuss the Rhineland (Chapter 3.2), *Anschluss* and Munich (Chapter 4.2 and 4.3 respectively), as well as Prague, the Soviet Pact and Poland. It is interesting to note that the timing of practically all of these events was not of Hitler's making, but that they were all long-term aims of the dictator.

There is some suggestion in essay 2 that Munich was indeed 'peace for our time' but you will no doubt wish to challenge that assumption. Paragraphs should then follow on i) Britain's change of policy, ii) Hitler's determination, iii) the Nazi-Soviet Pact (but primarily on its impact on Hitler's thinking) and iv) the attack on Poland. Essay 3 is not dissimilar in the sense that it requires you to go over much of the same ground, but it requires you to accept or reject the critical judgement about Munich and it also requires you to look in more detail at the Nazi-Soviet pact both from Hitler's and the democracies' point of view. Hitler felt the Pact meant there would be no war because Britain and France could do nothing about Poland; however, for Britain and France, Poland was not the main issue.

Source-based questions on 'The Outbreak of War'

1. Soviet and British perspectives on the growing crisis

Study the cartoons on pages 94 and 96. Answer the following questions:

a) What is the Soviet concern expressed in the cartoon on page 94? (4 marks)
b) What is Low's message in the cartoon on page 96? What is the significance of the figure on the floor? (6 marks)
c) Explain the bias of the cartoonists and consider whether or not it makes their cartoons invalid. (10 marks)

Structured Question on 'The Outbreak of War'

a) Why did Britain and France 'guarantee' Poland? (4 marks)
b) Outline why the Soviets made a pact with Hitler. (6 marks)
c) Explain why Hitler felt there would not be a general war over Poland. (10 marks)

Summary Diagram
The Outbreak of War

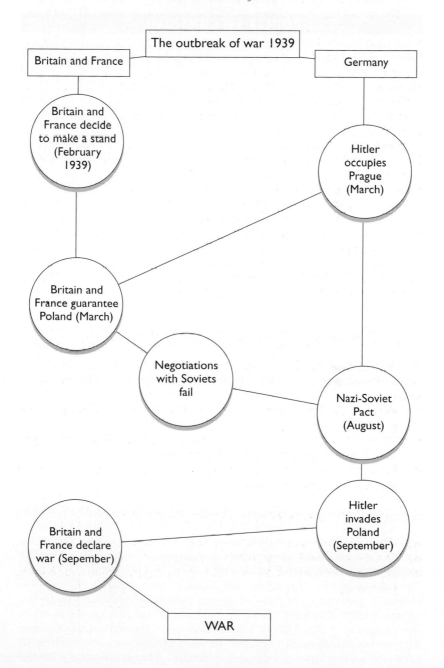

7 War

This chapter deals with Hitler's successful campaign in the west in 1940, his failure to resolve matters with Britain and his decision to launch a full-scale invasion of Russia. You should consider why Hitler turned on the Soviet Union before he had defeated Great Britain and why he was so obsessed with the idea of an eastern campaign.

KEY DATES

1940 Hitler invades Denmark and Norway (April); Hitler invades Holland, Belgium and France (May); Italy enters war (June); France capitulates (June); Battle of Britain (July-September); Tripartite Pact between Germany, Italy and Japan (September); Italy invades Greece and Egypt (October); Italians unsuccessful.

1941 Germany invades Yugoslavia and Greece (April-May); Germany invades the Soviet Union (June)

1 War in the West

KEY ISSUE In what way was Hitler's success in the west a diversion?

The events of September 1939 to June 1941 may be briefly stated. The Germans won a rapid and overwhelming victory in Poland (fighting was over by October 5th) and, following a new partition deal with the USSR, much of Poland was annexed (October 8th) and the rest subjected to a ruthless Germanization involving slave labour and racial extermination. Hitler set out to destroy the people and ultimately replace them by Germans.

In the West, Britain and France adopted an inactive and defensive role (often described as 'the Phoney War' though there were some attempts at economic warfare). In this sense, Britain and France did not really go to war at all in 1939. The guarantee to Poland had been a bluff and there was nothing the allies could do to help. Hitler on the other hand told his generals as early as 27 September that he intended an early attack in the West. On 18 October he approved Operation Yellow, the attack on France and the Low Countries. However, poor weather constantly postponed the attack through the winter, which also led to what turned out to be crucial revisions in the plan. On 8 April 1940 Hitler attacked Denmark and Norway. This was a sideshow, a response to allied plans to cut off Swedish iron ore rather than a German initiative. The main attack in the

West took place on 10 May and it was an astonishing success: the Dutch were defeated in a week, the Belgians in three weeks, the French in six. By the end of June it was all over. The speed of the victories took everyone by surprise - including the German High Command, the German government, and even Hitler himself. The opposing forces had been about roughly equal but the allies had been defeated by the superior skill, strategy and speed of their German opponents - which was just as well (from their point of view) because *blitzkrieg* (lightning war) was the only type of war that the Germans were really equipped for.

German policy in the West did not follow any preconceived blue-print and the rapidity of the victory caught Hitler out. He had no plans worked out, though there were elements of continuity with German aims in the First World War (drawn up in Bethmann Hollweg's September Programme of 1914). The army occupied the Low Countries (Holland, Belgium, Luxemburg) and most of France, and the economies of these countries were placed under German control.

Hitler did not know what to do about Britain. He expected the British to ask for peace terms and he was disappointed when he heard nothing. He finally made a vague appeal for peace on 19 July in which he stated: 'I can see no reason why this war should go on,'[1] but Britain did not respond. Chamberlain had been replaced by Winston Churchill as Prime Minister on May 10th, and eventually he brought to British policy a dogged determination to resist, though many in the cabinet (especially Chamberlain and Halifax) were in favour of exploring the possibilities of a settlement.

Hitler ordered plans for an invasion of Britain (Operation Sea Lion drawn up on July 16th) but these were always half-hearted, fraught with technical difficulties (German forces had not been built up for this task) and, once the Luftwaffe had failed to achieve air superiority in the Battle of Britain, were quietly dropped.

After the failure of the direct approach, Hitler toyed with the idea of an indirect approach against British interests in the Mediterranean (Mussolini had opened up this theatre by declaring war on June 10th) but Spain and Italy were not cooperative: Franco made impossible demands and the Afrika Korps was only formed and despatched in February 1941 when the Italians got into trouble. Admiral Raeder's plan (of 26 September 1940) to strike at Gibraltar and the Suez Canal was not put into action though a Tripartite Agreement between Italy, Germany and Japan signed on 27 September 1940, was designed to put further pressure on Britain to make peace.

2 Barbarossa

> KEY ISSUE Was this plan the culmination of all Hitler's aims and ambitions?

In truth Hitler's thoughts had once again turned to what had always been his principal aim - an attack on the Soviet Union. As early as 2 July 1940 he told his generals that now his hands were free 'for his great and proper task: the conflict with Bolshevism.'[2] Planning began in August and Operation Barbarossa was finally initiated on 18 December 1940. This was his grand design, his ultimate goal. The scale of the military preparations and the time and energy devoted to them put Barbarossa in a different category to all Hitler's other operations. That it was his ultimate goal can be gleaned from all his writings and conversations with Nazi and service leaders over a long period of time, dating back to *Mein Kampf* (written in 1924). Hitler had other plans but he could drop them and, as we have indicated, he could also be an opportunist - but he only took opportunities that appealed to him. For instance, the (very favourable) opportunities to strike at Britain in the Mediterranean and the Middle East in 1940 and 1941 did not interest him at all. The war with the Soviet Union was his principal aim and it was one of ideology and race - these factors also explain his ambivalence towards the British, whom he regarded as fellow Aryans.

Of course, there were vacillations over the attack on Russia, but generally speaking relations with the Russians steadily deteriorated. Stalin himself had not stood idly by - he waged a not too successful war against the Finns between November 1939 and March 1940 - and in July 1940, shocked and worried by Hitler's rapid victory in the West, he annexed the Baltic states. After this, disagreements grew over Rumania, Finland and Bulgaria, though this friction mainly came from Germany encroaching upon the Soviet sphere of influence. Germany valued these countries' raw materials - Rumania's oil in particular. Yet economic relations between Germany and Russia remained good and the Soviets were scrupulous in their supply of oil and raw materials. Stalin did not want to upset Hitler. Hitler met with Molotov on 12 November 1940 and may have been prepared to postpone his grand design for a while, but the meeting convinced him that the Russians would not accept German hegemony in Europe and that any kind of peaceful co-existence with the Soviets was impossible. He did not respond to a subsequent set of Russian demands and he stepped up the preparations for an all-out assault.

He was diverted briefly from his task in April and May 1941 when German forces had to take over Yugoslavia and Greece after the Italians had once again got into difficulties. However, Hitler would not be deflected from his main purpose, despite the Mediterranean opportunities after the capture of Crete and despite the fact that these excursions resulted in a four week delay in launching the assault on Russia.

Hitler had decided to leave Britain in isolation while he destroyed the Soviet Union. He (justifiably) discounted the possibility of a British attack and he was not yet in a position to confront Britain on a global basis. Moreover, he felt that the conquest of Russia would not only supply Germany with great economic resources and make her a truly world power, but it would also finally convince Britain of the impossibility of her position and bring her to the conference table.

The attack on the Soviet Union took place on June 22nd 1941. It was prepared over too long a time to be called opportunist. It was in fact, as we have already indicated, the culmination of all Hitler's obsessions - the desire to conquer living space, to capture raw materials, and to destroy Jewish-Bolshevism (as he called it). Moreover, due to the astonishing victories of 1940, the Führer was by now dangerously over-confident and he completely underestimated the scale of the Soviet Union and the resilience of her armed forces.

Arguably, then, this attack was the culmination of the whole process leading the continent of Europe into war and helps us put the events of 1935-39 in proper perspective. Of course this not the view of all historians. As we have suggested some contend that Hitler was responding to economic pressures, still others that military expansion developed a momentum of its own and that the Führer constantly needed to reinforce his leadership and popularity with ever more success. It can also be plausibly argued that the attack on the Soviet Union was brought about by a combination of Britain's unwillingness to make peace and Stalin's growing territorial ambitions. A statement in June 1940 after the collapse of France implies that Hitler had no immediate plans to invade Russia: 'there still remains the conflict with the East. That, however, is a task which throws up world-wide problems ... one might tackle it in ten years time, perhaps I shall leave it to my successor.'[3] However, the following month Britain's intransigence prompted him to remark: 'With Russia smashed, Britain's last hope would be shattered.'[4] However, a more effective way of bringing Britain to terms would have been to attack her interests in the Mediterranean and Middle East and, as we have already indicated, Hitler showed no interest in that strategy whatsoever. This thesis then - that Hitler only attacked Russia to force Britain to make peace - is not convincing. More convincing perhaps is the view that Russian ambitions were the cause of the attack. Hitler's meeting with Molotov in November made him wary - after Finland and the Baltic states, would the Soviets expand into the Balkans? Russia was expansionist and this could only lead to a clash. Yet we know Stalin had no plans to attack Nazi Germany and in the final analysis we cannot ignore the well-documented fact that Hitler had his own reasons for attacking the Soviet Union. Thus, on balance we revert to his hatred of 'Jewish

Bolshevism' and his obsession with *lebensraum* as much more likely explanations. Indeed Hitler's relief at having made the decision to attack Russia is palpable in this message to Mussolini on the morning of 21 June 1941:

> collaberation with the Soviet Union has ... been a heavy burden for me; for somehow it seemed to me a breach with my whole background, my views and my former obligations. I am happy to be rid of these spiritual torments.[5]

At last Hitler was about to embark on an obsession that, fortunately for humanity, proved to be his nemesis.

References
1 Noakes and Pridham, *Nazism*, p. 786.
2 Quoted in Fest, *Hitler*, p. 951.
3 Quoted in D.G. Williamson, *War and Peace: International Relations 1914-45* (Hodder, 1994), p. 131.
4 Quoted in Noakes and Pridham, *Nazism*, p. 791.
5 Quoted in Fest, *Hitler*, p. 961.
6 Quoted in William Shirer, *The Rise and Fall of the Third Reich* (Secker and Warburg, 1960), p. 1022.

Answering an essay question on 'War'

1. Why did Hitler invade the USSR in 1941?
If you accept that the invasion was the culmination of Hitler's aims and ambitions (and you do not have to - there are alternatives) then this essay requires you to go back all the way to *Mein Kampf*. You need to discuss the ideological basis for Hitler's attack on Russia (not just *lebensraum*, but the destruction of 'Jewish-Bolshevism') as well as his military position in 1941. Why did he feel that an undefeated Britain was not a problem? And why did he feel that the Soviet Union would collapse? He himself said: 'We have only to kick in the door and the whole rotten structure will come crashing down.'[6] Of course his previous success had made him over-confident and he believed *blitzkrieg* would lead to another Russian collapse and capitulation (as in 1917-18). The belief that history repeats itself is not an uncommon misconception among history students and dictators alike.

Summary Diagram
War

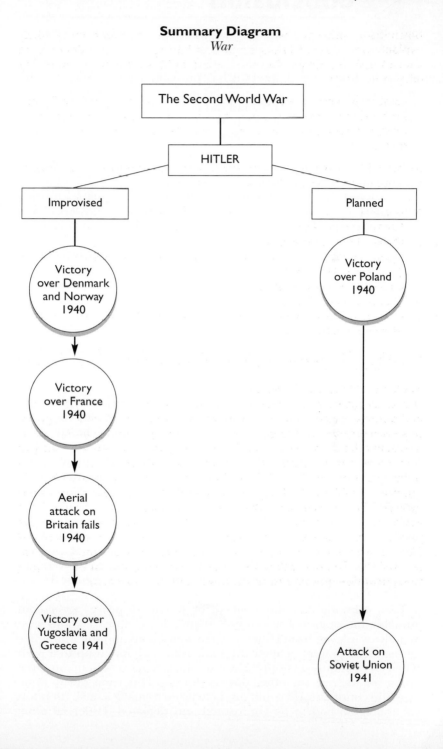

8 Conclusion

From the foregoing chapters it has probably been established that Britain did not want war; France did not want war; the Soviet Union did not want war; even Mussolini did not want war when it broke out. Of course Hitler himself did not want a major war in 1939, but it would be wrong to say he did not want war at all - he got the wrong war, that's all.

However, it would be too simple to ascribe the causes of the Second World War to just one man, since it was obviously the result of a wide variety of factors (of which Hitler was just one, but arguably the most important one). Undoubtedly the causes of the Second World War can be traced back to the consequences of the First. The collapse of four empires - German, Austrian, Russian and Ottoman - created a power vacuum in central and eastern Europe. Although Germany was beaten, she was not destroyed and undoubtedly possessed the potential power to revive and try to reverse the verdict. The disaffection of Germany together with the isolation of the Soviet Union, and more importantly, the isolation of what was arguably the world's most powerful nation, the United States of America, created an unstable international system policed by two old empires in decline, and Britain and France were not really up to the job - though ultimately they were prepared to make a stand to preserve their great power status.

The Second World War can also be traced back to the consequences of the Great Depression which brought Hitler to power. Indeed Hitler was in fact operating in a very favourable climate. As we have indicated, the international system was very unstable and he possessed some distinct advantages - he did not have to pay reparations and he was confronted by a pair of pacific democracies weakened by the recent economic collapse. However, he also demonstrated great skill in exploiting the situation, in particular with regard to Britain's ambivalence over the Treaty of Versailles and also by exploiting the principle of national self-determination for all that it was worth. In fact he was very successful up to 1939, at which point he started to allow his ideological obsessions of race and space to regain the upper hand in his decision-making. But it can be argued this was what he had been aiming to do all along.

Even allowing for the context of a flawed peace agreement, unstable international system and economic collapse, it would seem that the war arose from Hitler's expansionist aims and the willingness of the other powers to allow this expansion to happen up to a point when it could only be stopped by war. The Germans built up an offensive army whereas the other powers did not. Hitler was out to dominate the continent. He could not be trusted to make a deal, therefore eventually he had to be confronted and defeated. Hitler all along adhered to his major objective of acquiring '*Lebensraum* in the East,' though he was not committed to any specific policies for achieving it and throughout flexibility characterised his approach. That is why some historians have been able to dismiss the importance of *Mein Kampf*. But if *Mein Kampf* was not a blueprint, it certainly embodied his fundamental aims of race and space, aims he pursued with increasing fervour. Indeed as the war progressed ideology became more and more important - in the later stages, for instance, his racial war against the Jews seemed to take precedence over everything else as valuable rolling stock was used to transport Jews to the death camps instead of troops or weapons to war fronts.

Moreover, if we take a sympathetic approach to Appeasement, if we try to understand and explain British and French foreign policy; if we appreciate the difficulties their statesmen faced and their pacific intentions - then we cannot really blame them for the war, and we automatically revert to emphasising Hitler's responsibility once again. He alone wanted war. Of course not all historians do take a sympathetic approach to Appeasement. Some would suggest that the appeasers were guilty of wilful blindness, allowing Hitler too much and encouraging him to ask for more. However, yet others would argue that Hitler needed little encouragement because he had an agenda of his own. Whatever position one adopts on the origins of the Second World War, Hitler's centrality to the process cannot be denied, though of course he was not the only German who wanted to overthrow Versailles and reverse the verdict of the last war. The other Nazi leaders and the old imperial elite are not without blame, nor indeed are a large proportion of the German people: his foreign policy successes bound many of them to him. After all, he was only doing what the majority wanted him to do, exacting revenge for the humiliation and degradation many felt Germany had suffered since 1918. Indeed ordinary Germans came to develop a blind faith in his ability to do no wrong - to such an extent that he was able to lead them, like some pied piper, into a war in the East that the majority did not want. So whatever you decide, it remains a fact that Hitler attacked Poland, Hitler attacked Denmark and Norway; he attacked Holland, Belgium, Luxemburg and France; he also attacked Yugoslavia and Greece and finally he attacked Russia. No wonder the judges at the War Crimes Tribunal at Nuremberg did not have to agonise at length about where guilt lay.

But did the real war begin in 1939 or 1941? In a geographical sense there has always been some debate about whether it could rightfully be called a world war in 1939. Some suggest that initially it was just a European war (the European dimension has been the sole concern of this book), and that it did not become a world war until 1941 when Germany attacked the Soviet Union and the Japanese attacked the United States. Against this, it can be argued that Britain and France were global powers with global concerns and allies around the globe, which gave the conflict a 'world dimension' from the very beginning. Moreover, the adhesion of Italy in 1940 spread the fighting to Africa and the Middle East, which was clearly another indication of its global nature. And yet it does remain true to say that the war was clearly only a contest for European hegemony until 1941, which was, in any event, Hitler's fundamental aim (though he felt control of the continent would give him 'world power' status). But 1941 is an important date for another reason since it was not until Hitler attacked Russia in that year that his true ideological purpose was fully revealed. As he himself said just prior to the pact with Stalin on 11 August 1939 in a revealing statement to Carl Burckhardt, the League of Nations Commissioner in Danzig:

> Everything I undertake is directed against the Russians; if the West is too stupid and blind to grasp this, then I shall be compelled to come to an agreement with the Russians, beat the West, and then after their defeat turn against the Soviet Union with all my forces.[1]

And that of course is just what he did do. It would be fair to say that counterfactual speculation has little real validity in general but it could plausibly be argued in this case that if Hitler had not existed, then the Second World War might never have happened. But he did; and it did.

Reference
1   Quoted in Noakes and Pridham, *Nazism*, p. 739.

Further Reading

1 General

There are a myriad of books on the origins of the Second World War. The most successful in recent years, and probably the best, is P.M.H. Bell, *The Origins of the Second World War in Europe* (Longman, 1997), now in its second edition. Also good is Andrew J. Crozier, *The Causes of the Second World War* (Blackwell, 1997), which is strong on Appeasement and also covers the Pacific theatre - as does the small volume by R.J. Overy, *The Origins of the Second World War* (Longman, 2nd ed. 1998), which is largely thematic and has some documents. All these books have extensive bibliographies. For my review of them, see *History Review*, September 1998, p.55. Still well worth reading but often misleading is A.J.P. Taylor, *Origins of the Second World War* (Penguin, 1964).

2 Individual Countries

There are a number of useful volumes in Macmillan's *The Making of the Twentieth Century* series: in particular, Geoffrey Roberts, *The Soviet Union and the Origins of the Second World War* (1996); R.A.C. Parker, *Chamberlain and Appeasement: British Policy and the Coming of the Second World War* (1993); and Robert J. Young, *France and the Origins of the Second World War* (1996). The Macmillan volume on *Germany and the Origins of the Second World War* by Jonathan Wright had not appeared at the time of writing, but the number of books on Hitler and Nazism runs into hundreds if not thousands. Also useful on France is Anthony Adamthwaite, *Grandeur and Misery: France's bid for Power in Europe 1914-1940* (Arnold, 1995), and on the Soviet Union, G.F. Kennan, *Soviet Foreign Policy, 1917-41* (Greenwood Press, reprinted 1978).

For documentary sources and some useful analysis in between, J. Noakes and G. Pridham, *Nazism 1919-1945, Volume 3: Foreign Policy, War and Racial Extermination* (University of Exeter Press, 1988) is indispensable. William L. Shirer's *The Rise and Fall of the Third Reich* (Secker and Warburg, 1960) is still a useful quarry for information, but students are advised to be wary of the interpretation. On Hitler himself it seems likely that all works will be superceded by Ian Kershaw's projected two volume work, the first of which *Hitler 1889-1936: Hubris* (Allen Lane, 1998) appeared too late for this book. Kershaw has already written a short biography (Longman, 1991). Still useful are Alan Bullock, *Hitler, a Study in Tyranny* (Pelican, 1962), and Joachim C. Fest, *Hitler* (Weidenfeld and Nicolson, 1974). For an analysis of historical writings on Hitler see John Lukacs, *The Hitler of History* (Random House, 1997) and the review in *Teaching History*, No 94 by John D. Clare, pp. 43-47.

The following may also be consulted with some profit: William

Carr, *Arms, Autarky and Aggression. A Study in German Foreign Policy, 1933-39* (Arnold, reprinted 1979), John Hiden, *Germany and Europe,1919-39* (Longman 2nd ed., 1993), Richard Overy, *War and Economy in the Third Reich* (OUP, 1994), and G.L.Weinberg, *The Foreign Policy Of Hitler's Germany*, Vols. *I and II* (University of Chicago Press, 1970 and 1980).

3 Articles

Students are well advised to trawl through the back issues of *History Review, Modern History Review* and *New Perspective* for relevant articles on different aspects of this topic. For instance, Robert Pearce has written a pair of useful, short analyses on the Origins of the Second World War in *New Perspective*, December 1997, p. 25, and on Appeasement in *History Review*, March 1998, pp. 28-29. R.A.C. Parker has criticised Chamberlain in his article, 'Appeasing Hitler', *New Perspective*, March 1996, pp. 26-30; whereas John Garland has presented a more sympathetic portrayal in 'Neville Chamberlain', also in *New Perspective*, December 1998, pp. 30-34. A number of useful articles from the *Modern History Review* have been gathered together in *Europe 1914-1945*, edited by Peter Catterall and Richard Vinen (Heinemann, 1994).

Index